STUDENT
TO
SOCIETY

CARLY MACDONALD

STUDENT TO SOCIETY

LEADING STUDENTS TO THEIR PLACE IN SOCIETY

www.mascotbooks.com

Student to Society: Leading Students to Their Place in Society

For more information, please contact:
Mascot Books, an imprint of Amplify Publishing Group
620 Herndon Parkway, Suite 220
Herndon, VA 20170
info@mascotbooks.com

Library of Congress Control Number: 2025925985
CPSIA Code: PRV1125A
ISBN-13: 979-8-89138-836-9

Printed in the United States

To my mom, for leading me into society with life skills not taught in the classroom and for sitting with me at the kitchen table outlining items for this book.

To my lucky little Levi—there is a place for you in society. All you have to do is find your people, find a career that makes you happy to help people, and lead a life with an open heart.

CONTENTS

PURPOSE OF THIS BOOK

This book brings together students from all over the world who are facing the tough transition from student to society. Despite their different backgrounds, they all share the same emotions—excitement, uncertainty, and a bit of fear—as their world suddenly opens up after graduation. At its core, this book is a reminder that there's a place for everyone in society—it just takes some time (and a few growing pains) to find it.

I'm also here to remind you that deep down, you already know where you belong. Transitioning to society is attainable for everyone—it's a path we all have to walk at some point. This transition is universal and incredible.

ABOUT ME

It's important you get to know me before we dive into what I have to share to help you with this transition in life from student to society. To know me is to understand my parents' backgrounds first. Like everyone, I was influenced by the people around me, and that helped shape who I am today.

My dad is a successful certified public accountant (CPA) who has helped hundreds of self-made entrepreneurs create wealth for themselves and their families. He taught me everything I know about money. He always said if you can understand the money, you can understand the business. He's referencing the traditional way to evaluate a business: financial statements, different charts, and equations.

I always thought it was interesting how people made money to support themselves and their families. I was wildly impressed with everyone's skills and how they learned to earn money. In school I would always try to guess where my peers would end up. The class nerd becomes the doctor, the class comedian goes into sales, and the quiet one in the corner becomes a librarian. In reality, just ten-plus years out of school, you would be surprised who is doing what in society. How successful people become is determined not just by their book smarts but by their street smarts, too. I wanted to know how the rich became rich and how I could provide for myself and a family someday because all the adults out there just made it look easy.

I initially thought the trick to having a successful business was understanding financial statements. And yes, this is entirely true. This is why I earned both my bachelor's and master's degrees in accounting. I was milking the stay-in-school tactic as long as possible to have time to figure out where to go next. That's why I ended up going to graduate school. You need to understand your financial statements in order to grow your business, but that wasn't what my dad's clients were focused on. His clients' successes started with a small idea and focused on building teams around them to get them where they wanted to go. My dad was a very important part of their successes, but it was just one piece of their respective journeys. I quickly learned that there was more beyond the money—the people you surround yourself with determine your successes and failures.

My mom worked as an executive for a telephone company before deciding to be a stay-at-home mom to raise me. She made sure I was a well-rounded person in society by teaching me street smarts (life skills) not taught in the classroom. My mom was an executive before living her dream of being a mom. Her executive skills are unmatched—she's extremely organized, witty, and creative, all of which impacted me greatly growing up.

I like to think I am a good mix of both my mom and dad.

Like most of you, I had no idea what to do for a career. I figured I needed to maintain the lifestyle I had become accustomed to, so I decided to get an accounting degree.

I wanted to go into the accounting field because it was all I ever knew. It was in my DNA. I thought accounting was broad enough of a business major that I could transform it into anything later down the road as my career developed. Come to find out, writing a book is not a set of skills I learned with my accounting degree, but I am here doing it.

I also knew I wasn't your typical bland accountant because I had the personality of my mom. I always knew I was meant for something greater than simply following the path my parents had taken. I wanted to be my own entrepreneur, like my clients are. I have worked in public accounting for nine years now. I prepare tax returns for people in society who own their own businesses, including their individual returns and trust and estate returns. These are absolutely amazing people to surround yourself with. I basically would hang out with your local *Shark Tank* entrepreneurs. I essentially help clients generate wealth in their businesses by reading the financial statements from their businesses, and then I make sure their wealth grows and is transferred to their family members after they are gone. I deal with your typical millionaire neighbor. It's likely what you're dreaming of being someday. Think of me as your future advisor, here to tell you what I wish I knew at your age—and what my clients did early on to fast-track their success.

I have also taught various accounting courses for graduate and undergraduate students. At first, I pursued part-time teaching to pay off my car and keep me busy during the summer and fall months when work was slower. However, I slowly realized that I enjoyed it, and I wanted to provide an education to students that was practical and applicable. I wanted to teach on-the-job skills in the classroom. I was frustrated because, after twenty years in the classroom, I felt like I'd barely scratched the surface of what I actually needed to know to succeed in the workforce. I was challenged with the limited time as a professor to teach, review homework, and administer exams while providing real-world on-the-job learning content that the students would not get from a teacher who was not actively practicing accounting. I sat with this thought for a long time (years). Take it from me: Do not hold yourself back. I was my own worst enemy by not just taking more action and doing something about it. I wanted to help more kids on a more regional, maybe even global, scale than just my lucky thirty students that semester.

While I grew more frustrated at dealing with emails every morning, I started to write this book, finally. I understand the importance of having a license or letters after your name to validate your worth in an industry and being book smart to have skills to perform a job, but I realized that everyone's soft skills and street smarts are even more important to be successful. You can have all the licenses that you want, but it doesn't mean you are street smart, helpful to people, or know how to understand your business to create more wealth; it just means you are a good test-taker. I have a burning passion to help students enter society with skills, tools, and resources to help them thrive so they can be your low-key millionaire next door with the green grass.

INTRODUCTION

I'm glad you're here!

Seriously, I mean it. If you're reading this, you're already thinking about what comes next—and that's a big deal. This book is all about helping you navigate the leap from student life to the real world with a little less stress and a lot more confidence. Give me a chance. Try something new. Who knows, you might even finish a book. What? You . . . finish . . . reading a book . . . for fun? Just be patient with me. And yourself.

When you have been going to school your whole life, the transition from student to society is something that is not talked about enough *or* is overexplained to the point where it feels so all-consuming that it paralyzes you.

So, let's talk about it.

Congratulations! You're probably on the verge of graduating—or you just did. Whether it's high school, college, or another big step in your education, you're standing at the edge of what comes next.

At this time in your life, many adults will tell you to find a mentor in your industry—someone you can learn from and look to for guidance. Consider me one of the first mentors that you will have in your career. Be picky and selective in this endeavor. Your path will ultimately not look like anyone else's—it will be uniquely your own.

My advice in this book is different from everything you have ever learned before because it's well-rounded, sound advice that will make you feel like you have that "it" factor. You know, that factor that makes people stand out and be confident in a room full of people. It's the unspeakable qualities in someone that make them addicting to talk to or be around. The kind of person everyone loves being around and never tires of. That person has the "it" factor, and you can have it, too, through growing your own confidence in your job or career through this huge transition in life.

This book is designed to give you tips and tricks that you may already know, but with added context to figure out your next move. Its purpose is to provide you with friendly reminders, action items, and leading questions to guide you through this huge transition from student to society.

This book is packed with advice some parent figures might try to give you as you prepare for the real world. But let's be honest—you're more likely to take it in now because, well, I'm not them. I've never grounded you or lectured you about curfews, so we're already off to a great start.

This book was created with love and meant to provide direction and support for any student transitioning to society. Think about it: Students all over the world transition from student to society every year. So when it feels like it is crushing your world, know you are not alone, and we all have had to do it. It is the ultimate test of sink or swim. How do some have success and money in the bank later in life, and others have nothing to show for their hard work in society over the years?

As a student, your days follow a familiar routine—waking up early (hopefully remembering to brush your teeth and hair), rushing to catch the bus or walk to school, and then spending hours at a desk listening to lectures. And just when you think you're free, you head home to do even more work before dinner. Maybe sprinkle in a sport or activity here and there. But seriously, how does the American education system—or any country's—actually prepare students to participate in society?

How is memorizing a week of spelling words, remembering the Pythagorean theorem, or knowing that the mitochondria is the powerhouse of a cell that generates growth or energy useful as an adult? Aside from some very specific career choices, most of this subject matter will be irrelevant after you matriculate.

The same goes for a high school student transitioning to an advanced education student. Students are forced to claim an intensely focused, specific major as soon as possible in order to start taking core classes as part of that major's requirement for graduation. Although it feels like a huge accomplishment to know the major you want to study in college, unless you are building your personal skills, this major can also become irrelevant later on in your career. How is waking up later in the day, going to class in your sweatpants, getting lectured to, memorizing notes, and then doing whatever you want the rest of the time helpful to transitioning from student to society? How is your life as a student, which you sometimes dread, going to help you understand how to earn an income and teach you what to do with that income?

Don't you just salivate at the idea of having adult money and doing what you want with it? We all did at your age, and we all did something different with that money. You can really see it in someone's quality of life—how well they've managed their self-control with the money they earn as adults affects the opportunities they're able to give themselves. By the time you are long clear of your mid-twenties life crisis, you enter your midlife crisis (around your forties), where there are really only two paths. You have either set yourself up for retirement or not. Retirement sounds so fun and free, but how do adults get there? Why do some adults seem to work their whole lives without ever reaching retirement?

From the ages of three or four through high school or college, we are learning how to be professional students, not professionals in society. After graduating, we quickly realize we'll be learning for the rest of our lives, and most jobs are also spent sitting in an assigned seat all day.

Did you hear that? If you hate sitting at a desk now, you will REALLY hate sitting at a desk when you are an adult. Just imagine your adult body aching and rotting in a chair, EVEN IF you are paid top dollar to sit there. Choose your career with this in mind.

At some point—while sitting at a desk—I had a realization: If I was going to spend my life working at one, I might as well make a boatload of money doing it. Seemed logical at the time. But as I've since learned, that's not exactly the best way to go about actually making a lot of money. Yes, following your passions provides you with endless wealth! But you're not going to read about unicorns and rainbows here, and this isn't an overly encouraging book on how to do that. Remember I wanted to teach topics that were practical and that could be applied to a wide range of students.

If you're one of the lucky ones who's been at the same company for a while, maybe—just maybe—they'll get you a walking pad for your standing desk. At least then you won't be stuck miserably working all day, counting down the minutes until your commute home. Sound familiar? *YAY, you!* You can and should be teaching yourself new tricks outside of the classroom even if you are an old dog. Adapt or die!

Our grandparents didn't have computers growing up, and yet they are teaching themselves how to FaceTime you on your birthday while they are in Florida living their best lives in retirement with the money they saved from the careers they worked in for most of their lives. They might have had a lesson on how to learn how to use their smartphone at their community center, but they still get the credit for learning and adapting.

Can you imagine people sitting in a cafeteria learning how to use smartphones? Come on, there would be a funny old guy taking pictures of everyone, one asking for everyone's numbers, and also the serious learners . . . The list goes on. (Just like your current classroom.)

So why aren't these "common sense" transferable skills taught in school? Does anyone have common sense anymore? Can you be street smart and book smart? Why do students spend their lives on autopilot from birth through high school or college, only to suddenly be thrown into the world and expected to figure out how they fit into society? Why are students/individuals not self-thinkers? Why are you listening to your parent figures? I'll be honest—no judgment here. It's probably just because they're still paying for your life. Didn't you read the About Me section? I've been there, too. I didn't always listen to my parent figures either—and honestly, I still don't sometimes. Why does this all feel so new and uncomfortable?

I don't want to lose you so early! Sorry, parent figures! You have done a great job so far, and we will still listen to you and your advice and need you. A BIG BUT is coming—BUT we need to work together and start trusting the little intuitive voice that you've trained in our minds and make decisions for ourselves and our futures. Why am I comparing myself to others' social media projections of what they want me to think about them? Why is getting a job so hard to break through and stake my claim in society? Why do students have such a hard time transitioning from school to society?

Then your parent, relative, or summer reading program was right to give you this book if you've asked yourself one of these questions. I know. I'll admit it for you so you don't have to. It will hopefully be easier talking to me throughout this book than maybe the guidance counselor at school because I will come off as more relatable and (self-proclaimed) cool. We will decipher your purpose in society and make you think for yourself. So you can then go to all your amazing resources and use them effectively to get where you want to go.

While I was faced with these questions, I always came back to these questions: Why isn't anyone helping with transitions in life? Why isn't there any excitement around entering society other than walking across a stage? Yes, it's a milestone to walk across the stage, but where is the fun in this?

We all go through these milestones. We all experience similar things. We are all more similar than different. So, what's the big secret from students to society? What are these adults not telling us? What's the secret trick to being awesome at life? How do I build a life for myself that I can be proud of? How do I start this new chapter in my life off on the right foot? How did the wealthy do this?

I hope this book feels like an even closer friend—just like a favorite character from a show or a content creator you love following. I am here for you. We are all here for you. We all want the best for you and society. Let's connect the dots together to prove you do have the confidence to make this transition in life as smoothly as possible.

CHAPTER 1

CONNECTING STUDENT TO SOCIETY

You made it. Whether you just graduated, are staring down the next big step, or feel like your parent figures are shoving you off the edge of a cliff into adulthood—this moment is a turning point. Maybe you're celebrating, maybe you're panicking, or maybe you're just coasting through summer, wondering how long your graduation money will last.

Reality check: Society doesn't roll out a red carpet when you step into adulthood. There's no final celebration before life gets real. Instead, it can feel like running straight into a brick wall—one made of job applications, responsibilities, and the realization that money doesn't just appear in your bank account.

But before you write off everything you learned in school as useless, let's talk about how it actually connects to the world you're stepping into. The truth is, you've already been part of society—you just didn't realize it. And whether you loved school or felt like a prisoner counting down the days until graduation, the skills and experiences you've gained will shape the way you navigate what comes next. Let's break it down.

School Buildings vs. Office Buildings: More Alike Than You'd Think

Let's first start with the building. Yes, the school building.

Your school building has a library, a main office for the principal, a gym, lockers, parking for cars and buses, desks, different classrooms, and a cafeteria, among the obvious. This setting is going to be familiar in the general sense to the majority of the companies that you will work in, believe it or not.

The big boss or CEO will have their own big office, just like the principal. People will drive themselves to work, or they will take public transportation. Nowadays, some office buildings have gyms and showers so you can work out before or after work. Everyone has their own space in an office building to store their pens and pencils, just as they would at their school desk, locker, or dorm room. Each team might have their own room or area within a company, just like your classroom. Typically, there's a cafeteria in the building, or there are small mom-and-pop restaurants close to the company's building so you can go off campus for lunch.

Even though you spent years in a school filled with colorful posters, teachers guiding you, and maybe a jungle gym at recess, the reality is that your future workplace isn't all that different. The setting may change, but the structure—the expectations, routines, and the way you navigate challenges—remains surprisingly similar. The only difference now is *you* are the adult walking around. So, you have that nailed down, check.

Secondly, in the adult world, even your time is structured similarly to how it was in school. We all still have our morning routines, and we all commute to our jobs, just like we had to get up and get to school on time. Then there would be attendance in school, and in the real world you have to clock in to start getting paid. Maybe in school you had a homeroom where your attendance would be taken. In the real world, no one is calling your parent figures to see where you are if you don't show up to work. They are calling you to wonder why you aren't in to make money. And they may question your employment if it becomes a habit.

In your new job, you will put your lunch in the refrigerator and walk to your desk to get organized and review emails before your day starts. In a traditional corporate job, your day will consist of meetings, lunch, walks, personal work, and team projects. Sound familiar?

As a student, you go from class to class, stopping at your locker for your materials while going to lunch, the library, or your extracurriculars during the day. Think of each class that you attended like it is one meeting, because that's what it really is, right? For example, in a full-time job you will meet with the manager for about forty-five minutes to an hour on a team project or topic, and then you're onto your next meeting after that. In between meetings, you'll go back to your desk and grab more supplies that you need for your next meeting—notes, your laptop, a charger, etc. This is the same way you go to your locker and put your books back from the class before and grab the materials you need for the next class.

Third, lunch is typically still thirty minutes when you have a full-time job. We all wish lunch was the entire day filled with laughing and socializing. Doesn't everybody feel like they eat way too fast because they didn't give us enough time when we were kids? Now we have this horrible bad habit of stuffing our faces in a short amount of time with the added stress that comes with balancing a lot of professional and personal commitments. It will be easy to not take this break and still be productive, but don't be a fool—no matter how stressed you are, make sure you take a few minutes for yourself. Lunch is still heavenly. Now imagine being an adult, expected to eat professionally in front of colleagues in the break room. Did you ever actually learn how to eat slowly, carry on a conversation, and remember to sip your water—all without making a mess or forgetting your manners? Don't forget the napkin!

Lunch is still everyone's favorite time slot of the day. We get to go to the lunchroom or get out of the office and eat with our work friends. Eating lunch with work friends is also networking. So book all the lunch dates you can! Get to know your colleagues; they have a lot to teach you, and you have a lot to offer them as well.

Organization, Sign-Offs, and the Power of Your Name

It's interesting how, when you really compare the structure of school to the real world, the similarities start to stand out. It might even make you reconsider the idea that school didn't prepare you for life beyond the classroom.

Take sustained silent reading (SSR, or "sit down, shut up, and read," as my brother called it), for example. You'd sit at your desk with a book (probably not one of your choosing), pretending to read while your mind wandered elsewhere. Maybe you flipped through the pages absentmindedly, counting down the minutes. Sound familiar?

Well, let me tell you something—we adults out here in society would kill to have twenty free minutes to read a book that is enjoyable with the community of other readers. Companies even sometimes have book clubs for their employees. So, yes, the same way some of you would volunteer to help out the teacher during sustained silent reading to get out of reading, in the real world, you sign up for a book club so you can get a free lunch and get out of working for an hour maybe once or twice a month. Oh, how the tables have turned.

It is honestly one of the best things that a company can do. It's so enriching. Just like your summer reading list in high school or college. I know you probably don't believe me. You're thinking, *How will I go from avoiding reading to reading a book a month?* Jeez, that's a lot to ask for. But just wait. All of the advanced learning that you will get outside of school will be through books, podcasts, and conversations.

In school, your teacher tried to teach you the importance of staying organized—or at least did their best, even if it wasn't your strong suit. Sometimes, teachers would dedicate time to cleaning and organizing your desk—an attempt to instill a habit of order. On the first day of school, you likely received an agenda book, either provided by the school or included in your supply list.

Here's another connection between student life and the real world: In your career, staying organized doesn't go away. Being organized is a life skill. Instead of an agenda book, you'll rely on a digital calendar—most likely linked to your work email. This is where your meetings will be scheduled, deadlines tracked, and important reminders set. Business lunches? Those go on the calendar, too.

Passion Isn't Optional—It's the Point

Hate to break it to you, but your agenda book isn't retiring just because you graduated. Hopefully you got plenty of practice with this skill in school—because you'll need it.

I'm going to ask you to think way back now. Did your teacher ever make your parent figures sign off on your homework in your agenda book or sign your physical homework sheets? The purpose of this was to make sure that the parent figure was aware of whatever you were responsible for completing for the next day. Believe it or not, your boss or manager will have to sign off on work that you do as well for approval. Budgets or expenses typically need approval or sign-off in most industries. Bosses will likely review your work before it is sent to a client as well. A good boss will give you feedback to work on for the next time you do the same project.

Similar to sign-offs, didn't you hate writing your name on every single piece of paper? It felt like the only reason you were going to school some days was to write your name on another assignment. Instead of writing your name in the workforce, you will most likely be signing off on work that you have done or on emails. The purpose is still the same—to give the person credit whose name is on the project, sign-off, or email.

> **ON-THE-JOB TIP:** Write all of the feedback you get into a notebook so when you are reviewing your own work on the next project, you have a checklist of action items to review before you submit it for the boss's review. This way your boss won't find the same mistakes happening over and over in your work. If you keep making the same mistakes, you don't progress and earn more money. You'll just really annoy your boss. This skill is hard because we don't practice it as students. We take a test and see what we got wrong, and then we are on to the next test.

Your name means something. Every single time you write your name on a piece of paper in school, remember that your name is destined for greatness. Your name is important. Your name is what separates you from everyone else. Take pride in writing your name on something that you worked hard on and that you deserve credit for, even if it feels like busywork.

I can almost promise you that every time you get busywork in school, there is a purpose for it. I can almost guarantee you that you will be assigned busywork at work, too. So do the assignment with pride because your name is going on it. Those busywork homework assignments turn into small projects at work that add up and lead to promotions the same way all that busywork at school adds up to a better grade and maybe even some knowledge.

In school, you actually study what you love to learn about. You also do better with a topic that you like. The same goes for the "real" world. You have to be passionate about whatever you do in life. You will have this burning feeling and desire to succeed in your career. If you don't have that feeling, then you're not where you are supposed to be. You will always put your best foot forward or go the extra mile when you genuinely enjoy what you do for work. We are all lifelong learners.

ON-THE-JOB TIP: News flash, if you can't do the small busywork assignments at work, your boss won't trust you to do the hard stuff or lead a team, which equals more money!

Yet another connection for a student transitioning into society is the reality of consequences. In school, if you do something wrong, there are different levels of how you can get in trouble. If it is less serious, sometimes you just have a somewhat uncomfortable discussion with your teacher; if it's a little bit more serious, maybe you get a written warning from the teacher; if it's more serious than that, maybe you get sent to the principal's office for a verbal warning and a phone call to your parents. Oh, but if you really screwed up, you were sent to the principal's office and got detention or suspension or were expelled. Maybe the town cops came to school to scare someone if they really screwed up.

In the adult world, depending on the severity of your mistake or wrongdoing, you will either get a verbal warning from a manager, a written warning that is stored in your file, or be fired from your job.

Whether you are a student in the classroom or you are an adult in an office, there are consequences to your actions. The consequences get worse the older you get. The number of warnings or talks becomes less and less, too.

What about the fun in learning? How many of you went on class field trips? Did you go to the city, Washington, DC, a science museum, or a history museum? Was it a day trip or a few days? Did you get to eat out for the day and not have cafeteria food? Well, some of you might have to travel for work. Work trips are fun, but they also entail—you got it—*work*. You stay at a hotel and go to conferences with peers to LEARN.

ON-THE-JOB TIP: If you get fired and they put something in front of you to sign, do not sign it immediately. These moments are highly emotional, and if you're not in a balanced state of mind, you may not fully assess what you're signing. Getting fired is an emotional event; even the best employees can get fired. I'd go out on a limb and say everyone gets fired once in their life. Remember, you are technically an "employee at will," just like you are a "student at will." My point is that you have the choice and the privilege to be in the community and to add value every day, whether that's at school or at work. You could be fired because of a wrongdoing, but you could also be fired because of layoffs or budget cuts with no fault of your own.

What feels like the biggest change you've ever had in your life is actually not as big of a change as it feels. No one's ever sat you down and compared the two to help ease your mind as you are becoming an adult. Change is good, but change is really hard, too. The next biggest change you'll probably have in your life is when you start a family, if you choose to do so. You will be covering the cost for yourself and someone else. You will have to manage your life and their life with scheduling doctors' appointments, day care, and vacations. Your responsibility will increase dramatically the same way it does when you transition from student to society.

The next connection: asking questions. Your responsibility in society when you are a student is to learn and to learn *how to learn.* It is a great privilege to be able to go to school and learn. Remember, employee at will, student at will. So, your responsibility as a student is to ask questions so you have a greater understanding of the information being presented to you.

You may not know it now, but when the teacher stops and asks if anyone has any questions before they move onto the next lesson, it is the greatest time of pause for active learning. In the working world, your boss might not even ask if you have any questions after explaining something new to you. They'll just expect you to start working and get it done quickly.

It is your responsibility to ask a question if you don't understand it the first time it's explained to you. In the working world, it is assumed it might take you a few times of practice before you nail a concept. So when the teacher or boss asks if you have any questions, ask a question even if it's to repeat what they said just to hear the information again. The responsibility is on you to practice being an active learner because it will only make you better and more skilled.

Let me give you an example of real-world active learners—quarterbacks. Have you ever watched a football game where the quarterback walks back to the bench and someone throws an iPad at them? The quarterback is watching the play that was just performed! They are actively trying to figure out how they can move the ball down the field faster and better so they can win the game. They are also researching the other team's strategies. Be the quarterback in the classroom now; start tomorrow and practice being that engaged employee at work. All those quarterbacks are super wealthy, too—do as the rich do.

Recall how if a question isn't asked, it's assumed that everyone in the room understands the concept that was just presented. The odds of that happening to full capacity the first time are slim to none. That's why teachers assign homework—so you can practice what you learned in class that day.

It is your job right now to be a student and learn on the job. **You will learn on the job, but you will need this skill.** It's amazing that you get to practice this skill and then reflect on it in a job interview. It really shows how engaged and eager to learn you are! The fact that you are teachable is so appealing to a company.

So the next time your teacher asks the question, do not do the "student stare," because a stare is not respected in the real world. It is assumed that you will ask follow-up questions. Once something is taught to you, and after you practice it a few times, it is understood you will be an expert in the topic.

Lastly, one thing that is similar and yet very different during this transition is how you are graded. Yes, as both a student and as an adult in the real world, you are graded on your output or level of work that you put in toward a project or a course. However, it is a little different out here.

As a student, at the end of the year, you get a grade for a class. Every school is a little different, but throughout the year, you might get progress reports on where you stand in a classroom. The same goes for when you are an employee. You get graded once a year at your annual review. There are a few people in your company who evaluate you on their own scoring requirements and give you feedback on where you succeeded and where you need improvement. It's imperative to understand how you will get graded in the real world THE SAME WAY it is important to understand how a teacher will grade you on an assignment.

In school, syllabus week is important—all the expectations are laid out for students to find success and understand the expectations. The same is true for onboarding weeks at new jobs—these are the first few weeks at a new job when your new employer sets you up for success by discussing processes, expectations, and other details with you.

ON-THE-JOB TIP: Be the nerd. Ask for the annual review format when you first start, and stick it right above your computer so you are reminded daily of the high standards expected of you. Your annual review reflects the salary increase that you will get. If you did really well in a class or on an assignment, you earned yourself an A. You would feel good after you got an A and not so great if you got a D or an F. You would feel vindicated that your hard work was acknowledged when you received this great letter. You would even feel the best because you knew you were one of the top students in the class.

Then you enter the workforce. Showing up every day to a job that feels so different from the classroom—without a clear sense of where you stand—can be disorienting. It is the strangest feeling, walking into work and not getting a grade for the work you did the day before. You will not understand what I'm talking about until you go through the transition. It is so bizarre to not be evaluated and not understand your standing within the office on a daily or weekly basis because you are not receiving regular feedback. However, you should be prepared to receive other types of feedback that are not part of your annual review, like verbal and informal feedback.

In school, you received homework and weekly grades to measure your understanding of the material. In the working world, there's no nightly assignment being graded to show how you're performing compared to your peers. Instead, feedback is less frequent—often, no news is good news. As long as you're not being called into a meeting for a serious conversation or weekly check-ins with your boss, you're likely doing fine and will continue receiving your paycheck.

> ON-THE-JOB TIP: Take stock of that feedback and write it down as a note for when you have to reflect on your annual review. This way you can reference actual examples of when you performed well as a tool to help you negotiate that annual pay increase. You will also want to keep examples handy on ways to improve.

However, if you do get called in for feedback or a correction, handle it professionally. Take responsibility, acknowledge the issue, and focus on improving. Don't panic—just adjust and keep doing what you do best. After all, you've already put in the work in school, and that same effort will serve you well in your career.

Transitioning to a professional environment also means you'll be working with people and teams that have a wide range of experience. On team projects, there will likely be several generations represented. For years, you were surrounded by peers your age and took direction from teachers who were once students. In the workplace, you'll take direction from managers who were once individual contributors like you.

Your first interactions in this new environment might feel overwhelming—you'll want to prove yourself, yet part of you may long for the simplicity of recess. But you already have transferable skills. Someone taught you how to communicate with adults, and that foundation will serve you well.

We've established the parallels between school and the real world, but success goes beyond just getting by. Some of the most valuable workplace skills aren't graded in school, yet they make a huge impact.

So, how do you earn an A in the real world? One of the biggest measures of success is a referral—when a client, colleague, or associate is so satisfied with your work that they recommend you to someone else.

Here's the formula: **Hone your skills. → Deliver great results. → Create happy customers and employers. → Attract new opportunities. → Earn more money.**

So, how do you build a strong reputation and earn repeat business? It's simpler than you think—and it starts with embodying the right qualities.

1. **Polite.** Being polite goes a long way in life. There is a saying: "You can catch more flies with honey than vinegar." If you are sweet and courteous, people will want to work with you.
2. **Hardworking.** Yes, busywork still exists in the workplace—unbelievable, right? But here's the reality: Employers are paying for your time, and they expect to make the most of those forty (plus) hours a week.
3. **Punctual.** No one likes it when you waste their time. So, if you are going to be late for a reasonable reason, then communicate it as soon as you know to show that you are courteous of their time.
4. **Reliable.** If you say you are going to do something, you do it, and you do it 110 percent. Be a YES employee.

5. **Good listener.** You've practiced being a good listener in school, and the same skill applies in business meetings. Don't get distracted or disengaged—closing your laptop early is the equivalent of shutting a book in class. Be present and active, earning your paycheck with pride and leaving a positive impression.
6. **Imaginative.** Get off the screens and live. We are often layered with screens. You have your TV on, with your laptop on the coffee table, while looking at your phone doom scrolling. I hate to break it to you, but this does not provide added value to your future or life. Simply get off your screens and start thinking of how to solve a problem or how to start a side hustle. That's where success starts.
7. **Positivity.** While you can't control everything that happens, you *can* control how you respond. Maintaining a positive outlook—even in challenging situations—helps build trust, resilience, and forward momentum. Clients and colleagues are more likely to engage with someone who brings constructive energy to the table.
8. **Accuracy.** Always review your work before submitting it. Imagine you're being paid to find mistakes—that's the mindset I use to improve my work. If you're interning, your boss will likely assign you tasks to check their work for errors. This is a great opportunity to practice the same skill you already use when reviewing your homework.
9. **Skill.** Talent and skill go hand in hand. While talent is natural, skill is learned—whether through school, work, or personal pursuits like reading and education. If you don't have the natural talent for something, don't worry; with hard work, you can develop the skill you need to succeed. If you

start your own business, you'll quickly discover what you're good at and what you're not. These gaps are opportunities to hire people with the expertise you lack. It's a humbling experience, but recognizing what you don't know is key to growth.

10. **Open.** Great ideas can come from anywhere—they don't have to be yours. Limiting yourself, whether professionally or personally, will only hold you back. Don't stay in your comfort zone just because it's familiar. To truly succeed, sometimes you have to be fearless and embrace new challenges.

ON-THE-JOB TIP: Summarizing key points or concluding a meeting effectively is a transferable skill you'll need to develop and carry into the professional world. It seems so simple. When you are providing a service to a client or customer, it is important to express your added value to them and remind them of how far your relationship has come with them. For instance, before sending the bill for services rendered, professionals express the added value and how the service has enhanced their quality of life or ease of doing business. It is important to highlight this for people so they understand your hard work has only helped them. Then, when you send the bill, they'll be more inclined to pay on time—and with appreciation for the value you provided. If you don't have a final review or don't remind people what added value something is to them, they likely won't be able to make the connection on their own.

Now you know entering society has similarities to your environment right now, and continuing to make those connections will only help you transition and feel at ease with your world opening up.

One thing that isn't drilled into our heads as students is money management. Quite frankly, that's because some people in society get paid the big bucks to do this for wealthy clients. You would want to learn this from someone like them, not from a textbook.

Similar to a final in school, in the professional world you do all of the heavy lifting when it comes to refreshing your brain on what has been covered throughout the entire year. It is in your best interest to review what you have learned and take the key highlights with you to your next stage in your career or schooling. Luckily, I have given you SparkNotes at the end of each chapter. It is a fantastic time to reflect and see how much you have learned and grown in a short amount of time.

KEY TAKEAWAYS

- **You've Already Been Part of Society.** Your school days weren't just about memorizing facts—they were preparing you for life beyond the classroom. Whether it was managing schedules, collaborating in teams, or even eating lunch with others, these skills are the foundation for your adult life and work.
- **Passion Powers Progress.** Don't settle for a job that doesn't spark your passion. Just like school subjects that caught your interest, finding something you genuinely care about in your career will fuel your success. Your enthusiasm will drive you to put in the extra effort and continuously grow.
- **Consequences Matter—From Homework to Work.** Whether it's homework or work projects, your name is on the line. Just like in school, your work will be evaluated, and the quality of what you produce impacts your future. The same principles apply—take pride in your work and always strive to improve, even when it feels like "busywork."

CHAPTER 2

MONEY MANAGEMENT

Let's transition from similarities in the classroom to money management. As mentioned, the same way you get a syllabus the first day of class, you will receive an employment package your first day of your job. Both a school syllabus and an employment package are FULL of expectations for your performance.

In your employment package, you'll find a W-4 form. Picture this: You've just filled out your first W-4 form for withholdings on your paycheck, you work your first week at your adult job, and you smile ear to ear on Friday when you get a notification that your first paycheck has hit your checking account through the direct deposit you set up on your first day. So, what do you do? Everyone seems to have a budget or at least talks about a budget. But you just received your first paycheck from your first full-time job, and you're supposed to spend it on all of the adult things, right? You might also be wondering if you can just spend some of it and save later . . .

Quiet Wealth & Loud Spending

If you had a personal finance class in high school, can you recall a lesson that taught you what to do with your first paycheck? Did you fill out the W-4 form correctly? Did you even realize that form lets you indicate how you'd like your taxes to be withheld? Were you aware that the government takes out taxes from money you earn before you access it? All of these details can be overwhelming, and they're not always explained clearly or at all in high school or even college courses. You may be wondering, *What else did I not learn?*

> ON-THE-JOB TIP: When you submit your forms back to human resources, allow some time to review the forms with them in order to ensure you filled them out correctly. For the W-4 form, you will want to send your accountant a copy of your first pay stub to ensure the correct withholdings are taken out. You will likely do this every time you change jobs to ensure your withholdings are correct.

If you're starting to realize how much you *didn't* learn about managing your money, you're not alone. Most people enter the workforce with little guidance on how to set themselves up for long-term financial security. One of the smartest moves you can make early on? Start off by contributing enough to get the full employer match on your retirement plan. Once you're able to do that, increase your contribution by 2 percent each year until you hit the maximum. Two percent a year? You won't even feel it—but your future self will thank you. At the very least, not contributing to the match is leaving free money on the table. And if you're still living at home or your expenses are low, consider maxing out that 401(k) right away. Let those pre-tax dollars go to work for you in the stock market now, while time is on your side.

Money talks, and wealth whispers. Usually, when someone speaks loudly and often about all the money and material items they have, they likely aren't that well off. They may have a lot of debt if they just talk about their awesome house and their awesome car because they most likely took a loan out to obtain them. Let me tell you something: Unless those things were paid for in cash, then the bank owns them. They are liabilities, not assets. An asset is something of value or something that generates value for you. A liability is something that costs money or an expense.

Debt can be debilitating. Start good habits now. Do not get yourself into a ton of bad debt. Credit card debt and student loan debt are among the worst. Ideally you should be paying off your credit card every month with the money you earned at your job while living below your means. If you can't manage a credit card responsibly, then you should cancel the card or not make expensive decisions that can impact your financial freedom to retire one day.

The people who have wealth—accumulated, sustained financial stability—don't often talk about it. That's how much money they have. That is the type of rich you want to be. Real wealthy people don't brag about how much stuff or money they have.

Well, that's called having *class*. Class gets you very, very far in life. Class is not reclining on an airplane into someone else's lap. I know . . . It's a very controversial topic. It's a common courtesy for other patrons in society. Class is not loudly sharing how wealthy you are. Real wealthy people are not going around saying how much their car costs or how much their jewelry is. If you are really wealthy or have a taste for those materialistic items, then you know how much they cost, and nothing needs to actually be said.

Even if you have all the money in the world, it doesn't mean you're a good person or have class.

Spending vs. Saving: Starting Strong

Budgeting, saving, and living below your means is all you need to do. It's that simple. Don't overcomplicate it like everyone else.

Let's set the scene: You are a young twentysomething. You (1) made the decision to go into a trade; (2) decided to go right to work after high school; or (3) decided to get an advanced degree for either two, four, or more years of schooling. Regardless of the decision or a passion that you are chasing, you are going to start earning adult money, whether it's from a summer internship or you're starting your apprentice hours.

Side Bar: I want to make something crystal clear. Whatever you do after high school is fantastic in respect to furthering your education. College is not for everybody. Think about it: College *is* a trade school. You are supposed to be there to learn a skill and use that skill once you enter the real world. Just like an electrician learns a skill and has apprentice work to practice under someone working in the real world and hopefully gets a full-time job after. In college, you learn a skill in the classroom, and you apply for internships, which are apprenticeships, to hopefully score that employment package. When touring colleges, it is important to analyze their programs not how cool the school is or how cool it will make you look. Trade schools are a fantastic way to learn a skill and earn a living, and so are colleges.

You have never seen this much money deposited into your checking account before. Unless you had a rich aunt who left you a huge inheritance, this is the most money that has come your way. Of course, when you first get this money, you're going to want to go on a small (or big) shopping spree. This will happen to you when you get a promotion at your job in the future as well. There will be newfound money to be spent on fun stuff for yourself . . . but not so fast!

You want to be rich. You want to be successful. You want to have assets. *You want to be wealthy*. At sixty, you want to have something to show for all these years of hard work, right?

Living our lives and having happiness is important, too. So yes, go ahead and buy yourself a new outfit, a new car, or a new watch to reward yourself. But make sure your choices are WITHIN REASON, considering your financial situation. Expecting you to not spend any of this newfound cash on something fun and rewarding would be wildly unrealistic. I need to be honest with you though . . . Just knowing you can afford something or can reward yourself since you aren't getting a grade anymore is important. It is almost MORE IMPORTANT than the instant gratification that the item will give you. We are all natural spenders. We are trying to instill good money management habits in you at a young age so you get addicted to saving money and watching your assets grow rather than watching all your stuff grow. Demonstrating that discipline is knowing a need versus a want.

But are you putting yourself on a budget, either paycheck to paycheck or month by month? Are you actually understanding where you were spending your money? Are you slowly acquiring assets and managing your liabilities?

It probably goes either of two ways: you either make a very detailed Excel sheet with charts and pivot tables of your spending habits, or you spend like a drunken sailor, barely checking your accounts. Both are probably unreasonable, so finding somewhere in the middle is the best place to be.

When budgeting, you have to keep your goals in mind. You save money in order to invest in your future the same way you eat vegetables to invest in your health, so by the time you're sixty, you are happy, healthy, and rich, honey!

Building a Budget for Your Future Self

It's very simple—once you get your first job, work hard to keep the job and stay employed. If it is possible for you, the best option is to live at home as long as you can and enjoy your parent figures and spend time with them.

While you are living at home—and possibly hating your life because you just went from living with your friends to losing that community and coming home to the cruel world of society—you start pretending like you are paying rent or a car payment if you need a new car.

Most likely, your parent figures are buying the toilet paper, electricity, water, and heat, which you will soon be paying for the second you move out. So, start practicing paying for that now. Put this money in an account where it is not as easy to access or see day-to-day, so it is funded and working hard for you. This money should be invested into a brokerage account, not just a savings account. It's all about maximizing your dollar and putting your money to work for you. Each month, the second you get your paycheck, you pay off your credit card, pay your rent, and pay toward your future. You need to pay for your future self first, the same way you would pay yourself first if you owned your own company. There is no way you would leave the same amount of money in your account unspent at the end of the month to be saved if you didn't pull it right away and pretend it was another bill. You would spend it. I would spend it. We would all find a way to spend that money even if we didn't necessarily need to spend it on something important. Then you live off what's left of the paycheck until the next pay period. Sounds simple, right? Almost too simple. Save money, invest in diversification, and let time compound.

What you need to understand now is that at any age and at any income level, it feels hard to save just some of it for your future self. You will always find an excuse to spend newfound funds. So start while you are young so you can take advantage of compounding interest. When you are young, establish a routine of consistently growing your wealth. If you think it's too hard, you are just giving yourself an excuse to not start. Shame on you and your future self. The same goes for finding an excuse to not eat vegetables.

Side Bar: It is a privilege to live on a college campus, graduate, and have a family to move in with after school. It is also rather harsh to go from the highs of the senior slide and all of the events that happen before graduation to the abrupt halt and quietness of living in your childhood bedroom, where all your freedoms feel like they have been taken away. (I'm here to remind you they have not, and you're not the only one who feels like that.)

Some parent figures might not let you move back in, which is totally reasonable! For others, it may not be a good choice for you for many reasons. They raised you and hopefully have had these conversations with you for a while to lead up to you moving out after graduation. You probably received pots and pans for the holidays over the past few years. They really stuck it to you if they did that. You better be awfully grateful they bought the pans so you didn't have to.

If you want to be treated like an adult, have the adult conversation and ask what the expectations are after graduation. Your parent figures will greatly appreciate you stepping up to the plate and taking initiative. You say, "I want to live at home and save money and pretend to pay rent while I am still living under your roof so that I do not have to move back in with you when I am older. I want to set myself up for success, and I need a little more time to acquire assets so I have liquidity for a bank to give me a loan for a house or save for first and last rent or purchase a reliable car to get to work. Does this sound reasonable to you? Can we discuss a timeline that works for both of us?"

Yes, you heard that correctly. Nothing feels like a kick to the nuts more than having to suck up your pride and ask to move back into your parent figures' home AFTER you've spent all your adult money while you live with your friends in the city in your early twenties, going out to all the bars every other night and spending your whole paycheck. Again, you have nothing to show for your hard work (maybe other than some memories and some good networking opportunities). How soul-sucking is it to have your freedom taken away AGAIN?

Anyways, do you see what the idea is with this type of planned budgeting? You are building your next move into your budget. You are planning for your future self. You are saving your rent expense that you are anticipating in the coming years/months. So once this goal comes to fruition with a nice nest egg, you buy a house or move into an apartment or condo. You are already used to having that expense in your budget. HELLO! When you keep saving for the next thing in life, you might not even use the nest egg that you saved up. You will likely keep the nest egg invested in an asset while using the budgeted portion of your salary to actually level up in life. This way your assets are still working for you and growing while you are continuously managing your money. You just paid for your future goal of moving out and saved enough to move out, AND that amount you saved monthly goes toward that rent payment, which won't affect your spending habits because you were smart and built it in already. Personal financing is personal, and it will look different for everyone. But if you keep your fixed costs low and your goals in mind for your future, you will be all set. It is all about living below your means.

ON-THE-JOB TIP: Set a calendar reminder for when you are able to start contributing to your 401(k) and get back in touch with Human Resources to help you out. That's what they are there for. They will also help you pick the right health insurance plan for you.

Obviously, you can't budget for everything, because life can throw unexpected things at you. Having a little emergency fund is helpful, too. You don't want to put yourself in a position where you have to borrow or take money out early from your 401(k). That money is there working for you and should just be forgotten about until retirement is imminent. Period.

Let's take it a step further. After you saved money for a down payment on a house with all of your "rent money" that you had put to the side while you were living with your parent figures, you are now able to finally buy a house. This is because you've built up liquidity, which is one of the prerequisites the bank is looking for in order to give you a loan. Don't sleep on that sentence. The bank is looking at your personal balance sheet to see how liquid you are (how many assets you have) in order to guarantee you a loan. This is where your personal balance sheet comes in. Just like a business tracks its financial health, you should, too. It's time to understand exactly where you stand—what you own, what you owe, and how that picture will evolve over time.

Personal Balance Sheet

Use the table on the next page to create your personal balance sheet. At the top, list all of your *assets*—everything you own. At the bottom, list your *liabilities*—everything you owe. This format mirrors a company's balance sheet and reflects the idea that managing your personal finances like a business can help build long-term stability. You are illustrating with this chart a picture of your WHOLE wealth.

Your personal balance sheet connects to your tax return—something we'll cover in Chapter 3: Cost of Living, Career Choices, and Creating a Life You Can Afford. As a student, your current assets may be limited, but this exercise is about building awareness and planning for growth. I've provided a blank chart for you to complete, along with an example version to help guide you.

Personal Balance Sheet for YOU Currently
Assets:
Liabilities:

Personal Balance Sheet for YOU Currently
Assets: Salary from Summer Job ~$7,000 Checking Account ~$200 Savings Account from Parent Figures ~$3,000 Car, Scooter, or Bike ~$5,000
Liabilities: Student Loans ~$75,000 Cost of Living Expenses ~$350/Month

This habit of checking in on your financial health each year—just like the wealthy do—will help you stay in control of your money, make informed decisions, and build quiet wealth. You don't need to be perfect. You just need to get started and stay consistent. Let's keep building from here.

Building from Here

Your next goal is probably having children with a significant other. This is probably the next big expense and transition in life. And if it's not, you can save for something else. Now that you are more established, you've probably gotten a raise at work in between this time, from living at your parent figures' home to now owning your own home, condominium, or apartment. Now you pretend you're paying day-care expenses to save up for your future family.

Depending on your combined income—and whether one of you is considering staying home with the kids as an alternative to paying for day care—I often recommend beginning to live off of just one income and saving the other entirely. I've seen many clients make this shift well before having children, giving themselves time to adjust their budget and soften the impact of eventually living on a single income. This approach isn't just for the wealthy; it's a practical strategy I've seen families of all income levels use to prepare for a stay-at-home parent or a growing family while their children are young. Of course, this plan won't be right for everyone. If both spouses plan to keep working and continue contributing to their 401(k)s, that's absolutely okay, too.

Now, listen, I know budgeting for day care is often like paying a second mortgage—it's so expensive! If you want to start budgeting for day care before having kids, the exact cost doesn't matter—what's important is setting aside a significant amount so the expense is already built into your budget when the time comes. This day-care expense savings will most likely go toward random baby needs, college savings accounts, or a summer/day program. You've already done the work. You've already become an adult. You understand money management.

You were planning for your future and being smart with your money. Then you go to the next goal and budget for it after that. Are you getting that the only one who is going to hold you accountable and make this happen for yourself is you? Don't inherit any parent figures' bad habits around money.

News flash: This is what all the wealthy people are doing and letting their children do, and they also use this strategy to build up liquidity for their next business venture or next purchase within their business.

From Employee to Entrepreneur

Your income source is a very personal topic as well. Someone who is an entrepreneur, who owns their own business, and who sends out invoices to many different clients has many different sources of income. If they were to lose one client, it would not affect their business or their quality of life. Now, if someone who is an employee of a company that only receives a W-2 and gets a paycheck every two weeks loses that source of income, that would have a significant effect on their quality of life.

That's why so many people want to be entrepreneurs and own their own businesses. Entrepreneurship sounds sexy. They want security and knowing that they can go out and get more business or more income if they need it or have the flexibility and know that if a deal goes south, it won't rock the boat.

The goal of owning your own business usually takes time, and these skills are developed to run your own business by working for someone else first. Sometimes learning how not to do things is more informational than working at a business that runs smoothly. Learn from others' mistakes on the job. You have the intuition to know right from wrong, whether you follow it or not in your own life.

You will learn how you want to run your own business when you see others run theirs. We are lucky enough to live where we are able to earn as much as we want. Most of the time, people start spending a few hours a day to foster a side gig. Have you ever been asked, "You have a nine-to-five, but what's your five-to-nine (5:00 p.m. to 9:00 p.m.)? What's your side hustle?"

I want to make something SUPER clear about owning your own business. Sometimes this is the ultimate goal because you have had teachers and parent figures micromanage you up until this point, and you want to be free and make your own decisions. That's great.

BUT know that you are still accountable to people when you own your own business. You are collaborating with employees and/or clients, so you are not always making the decisions. I would argue that you are *more* accountable to a whole host of people when you own your own business compared to just one boss. You are accountable to IT, the bookkeeper, employees, insurance providers, office managers, and so on. Everyone needs you and your time all the time—not just from nine to five.

ON-THE-JOB TIP: You don't need to learn directly from the CEO of the company you intern/work for just to learn how to be successful. I think this might have been one of the biggest misunderstandings when I entered the workforce. I was twenty and wanted to be taken as seriously as the CEO, thirty years older than me. I'm laughing at this now, but I think it's a common mistake many make. From every boss, good or bad, you can gain the lessons you need to prepare for the next stage of your career.

There is a saying that some people

would rather work one hundred hours for themselves than forty hours a week for someone else. There are so many benefits to owning your own business, but there are significant risks and challenges as well.

The backbone of America relies on small businesses. I'm saying it is not as glamorous as it sounds, and the probability that you will graduate right away and have a business that you start successfully is slim . . . unless you are Mark Zuckerberg.

You need to be in this rut, this time of challenging yourself, this time of figuring it *all* out, and this time of learning and adapting to society before you make your millions working for yourself or a company. This transition from student to society is blah. It's just a lot. But you likely don't have the stresses or responsibilities of taking care of a baby. The only person who is relying on you is you. So take advantage of this time now.

Probably one of the most important lessons you will learn in your first job is that you want to have a job that takes care of you—not your parent figures, not your grandparents, not your boyfriend or girlfriend. Build confidence in yourself by developing skills both in and outside the classroom—the kind of skills that will empower you to thrive and earn in the real world. Having strong financial literacy gives you the confidence as well to move through life just a little easier. Yes, money buys the cars and the watches, but it really only buys you opportunities in life that you wouldn't be able to afford otherwise. Ensure your job gives you a social environment (like the classroom), financial security, confidence, happiness, and purpose. Your job as a student already gives you all of those things.

One step at a time. Trust the process. Climb the ladder. Grow your network. Manage your money. Learn who you are and the skills that you have to share with society. We have all been there, and we are all still working on it. There is no shame in the struggle when you are trying to get where you want to go in life.

KEY TAKEAWAYS

- **Wealth Is Quiet.** Just because someone has all the latest things doesn't mean they're financially secure. True wealth isn't always loud. As you grow and succeed, carry yourself with intention and class—it's not just about what you earn but how you manage and present it.
- **Start Strong, Start Smart.** The earlier you build smart habits, the more options you create for your future. Practice telling the difference between wants and needs. Just because you can buy something doesn't mean you should. Find your balance between spending and saving—it's personal and evolves over time.
- **Budget With Purpose.** A strong budget isn't just about tracking dollars—it's about planning your next step. Whether it's buying a car or moving out, make space for your goals in your budget. Prioritize liquidity so your money can move with you. Budgeting is a habit that builds momentum.

CHAPTER 3

COST OF LIVING, CAREER CHOICES & CREATING A LIFE YOU CAN AFFORD

Up until this point, it is likely your parent figures have covered your cost of living. Someone other than yourself has managed money for YOU. Whether they managed it well or poorly is another thing. They have paid for your food, shelter, clothes, new sneakers in August before school starts, and more.

In theory, some of you have started working part-time jobs or at least summer jobs as you have gotten older. Think of your personal balance sheet. You slowly start to realize . . . *it's expensive to be me.* Maybe one of your parent figures even joked when you were younger that you better marry rich because you are doomed otherwise. While this is extremely funny, I hope they started to instill habits so you could learn to cover the cost of living for yourself. This is something that is not taught in most schools, but you already have a sense of it. In fact, most of our money habits come from our parent figures UNLESS we do the work to teach ourselves good habits and tricks. Instilling good habits isn't the hard part—it's undoing the bad ones that takes real work. That's why the planned budgeting strategies from the last chapter and our focus on this age group matter so much. The goal is to replace unhealthy financial habits early—before they really take hold and while you're still just getting started. It's much easier to shape your mindset now than to try and change it later in your twenties.

Understanding the Tax Form and Retirement Connection

If you look at the first page of your tax return—formally known as Form 1040, the US Individual Income Tax Return, the form you or your accountant sends to the US government when you file taxes each year—I can provide a visual that can help explain retirement. The first line is wages and salary. This is the total income that you earned at your job during that year. In theory, this number keeps growing and getting larger and larger. It becomes even larger when you marry, and both of your incomes are on that one line if you choose to file a joint return. So, if you decide you want to marry, make sure you marry well—not necessarily for money. Hopefully your partner is gainfully employed, and you aren't covering the cost of their living expenses. Unless you want to. That's different.

The lines beneath this show all other types of income. This income (assets) is rental income, investment income, annuity income, social security income, Schedule C (for when you own your own business) income, and so on and so on. Once all that other income is equal to or greater than that first line of income, that's when clients can retire because they have enough money and other investment vehicles to cover their costs compared to their wage income. Over lifetimes, people watch their other assets other than their wages grow, and it is a major factor in deciding when and if ever to retire. It's a super personal decision to retire, and some, believe it or not, choose not to for reasons outside of financial considerations. Meaning, some still work because of the social factor or to stay on a schedule and be disciplined. Some that don't retire say, "How much golfing can I actually do every day? It becomes a chore." Believe it or not.

A Fresh Look at the Workweek

That brings me to another thought about how to look at income and covering fixed costs. Your fixed costs are your expenses in each pay period that you need to pay to cover your cost of living. We'll discuss fixed costs again in detail later, but some examples of fixed costs include rent, gym membership, food allowance, phone bill, car payment, student loan payments, etc. Your fixed costs are anything you need to live. It does not include any expenses beyond a reasonable lifestyle, like a boat, RV, expensive clothes, décor, etc. Understanding this distinction is especially important when you

ON-THE-JOB TIP: In case you want the workweek to go by painfully slowly by talking about what you are doing that weekend on Monday, know that typically in the lunchroom no one is talking about what they are doing that weekend until Wednesday. Monday is too busy with getting organized for the week, and Tuesday may be harder than Monday sometimes, but there's this rule that you don't really talk about what you're doing for the following weekend until Wednesday.

think about your weekend spending. In the adult world, weekends are often treated like mini-vacations—a mindset that can lead to lifestyle creep if you're not careful, especially if you work a typical nine-to-five job or forty hours a week.

I remember learning this rule once I started working, and someone said, "That's because we are slaves to society Monday and Tuesday. We are covering our cost of living in society as an adult. Between taxes, contributions to our 401(k), paying for our health insurance, and/ or childcare, we are essentially working for free at the beginning of the week for what is taken out of our paychecks. Then all the money we make on Thursdays and Fridays is essentially what we are able to spend and live off of after all necessary living expenses are paid for." I remember thinking that was a very depressing way to look at the workweek and that's probably why everybody hates Mondays, especially after their mini-vacations, but it was true! I find Mondays refreshing. A new start to the week. A reset to tasks that need to be handled. It's all how you look at life.

They also said they had that mindset because when they were in their early twenties, they were in school and working so they could pay off school while getting their degree. They would go to school in the mornings, and they would work at night and on weekends in a very fancy restaurant. Back then they didn't have their vacation weekends, so I think that's why they like to have their weekends open for whatever they want to do now. They always had the plan that they wanted to have fun every weekend, and I think that's a great lifestyle and perspective on life. They were told to cover their cost of living as they were working toward a career. "Fast cash" jobs are always a great idea to have to fall back on. Working in food and beverage is always a great SKILL to have and fall back on if, heaven forbid, you are in between jobs at some point in your life or just looking to earn a few extra dollars to make ends meet or meet a money-management goal faster.

ON-THE-JOB TIP: If you are wishing away your work week, you are in the wrong career or industry.

Budgeting & Psychology: It's Not Just About More Money

I'd argue that if you are trying to cover your cost of living/lifestyle, simply making more money won't solve your problems. It sounds like you need to revisit your budget and expenses. It sounds like you are living beyond your means. So yes, it is nice to want to work hard to get more money to do what you need to do in life, but are you growing your assets or just spending more money?

You are doing yourself a disservice if you think all you need to do is make more money while you are spending the majority of the money you already make. Why aren't you trying to save or invest some of the money you make? Your first goal should be to hold on to as much of the money you're already earning—instead of getting stuck on a hamster wheel, constantly chasing more income just to fund unnecessary indulgences. Yes, increasing your income is a goal eventually, but it shouldn't come at the expense of your time and well-being. After all, there are only so many hours in a week to work, rest, and actually enjoy life—and only so much overtime you can physically take on.

A good way to understand this concept is through the game of Monopoly. There are two types of players—and, by extension, two types of people in the real world. The first type moves around the board without ever buying properties or investments. They simply work, collect their $200 every time they pass Go, try to stay out of jail, and repeat the cycle—much like people who rely solely on a paycheck and never build wealth-generating assets.

Then there's the second type—the wealth builders. They buy properties early and steadily collect rent from others, growing their income passively as the game progresses. In real life, these are the people who invest wisely and generate income beyond their regular jobs.

Do you see how this ties back to your tax return? Some people only report a W-2—income from a single job. Others report a W-2 *and* additional income from investments, side businesses, or rental properties. That's the power of building assets—and stepping off the endless work-to-spend cycle.

The psychology of money is a very interesting thing. Yes, everyone worries about where they can earn their next dollar.

Choosing a Career That Supports Your Life

I think when you are young and trying to figure out what you want to do in life for a career, it's easy to think, *If I am going to sit at a desk all day, I want to be able to make as much money as I can.* I think that's a really common mindset at that age, because you don't know what you don't know, and the unknown is so unpredictable and uncomfortable. Not having complete control over your career and path feels insane. By taking the right steps, you can position yourself for success and inspire the generation before you to invest in your growth and earning potential.

The bottom line is don't pick a job based on how much money you are going to make. Yes, you obviously want to be able to cover the cost of your living expenses, but do not pick a career just to cover those expenses and a lavish lifestyle. You will be miserable forty-plus hours out of the week. That sounds horrible. If having a boat and enjoying it every weekend is your goal, then have that goal and **drive your ambitions with your earnings**. Or work on a charter boat and learn from someone else how they run their boat business so you can be out on the water every day instead of sitting at a desk. Don't just do it for the money, that's all. You will be able to make money at whatever you do as long as you work hard and keep yourself well-connected within your network and community.

When you are thinking about what you want to do for a career, you need to not only think about how much money you could possibly make to cover your life expenses, but you also need to think about the lifestyle you will have.

The story and exercise I am about to share will help you with this. Remember, your passions follow you. They are right in front of you. You will have to connect with yourself and quiet the noise in society to figure out where you best belong. No one else can do this for you. Your network can obviously help you, but you have the power to have whatever career you want in society. Leaving high school behind, you get to choose who you will be in society. You will have a new beginning. Remember, even people who have known you since you were young—like classmates you met in kindergarten—don't really know who you're meant to be in the world. Don't let others decide who you are in society or in the classroom going forward.

That's why it's so important to explore different paths and pay attention to the people around you who seem fulfilled by the choices they've made. I personally love going to the dentist. I love how clean my teeth feel after, even if it is a little bit of torture while you're sitting in the chair for an hour. The dental hygienist that I go to is one of the nicest, funniest, sweetest, and happiest people I have ever met. We got along great right from the start. During my appointments, obviously she talks to me, and I listen because she has her fingers in my mouth, but recently I asked her about what it took to be a dental hygienist. I think she loves her life and her job so much because she chose a lifestyle that would be flexible for her and her future. Some may just want to find a job that covers their cost of living, and that's fine. But everyone in society is allowed to have a career that is nourishing to them in a multifaceted way that enhances their quality of life.

She said she wasn't the greatest in school, so she knew she needed to go into some sort of trade. She also knew she couldn't afford to get into a lot of student debt either, so with the help of her parent figures, she went to a career fair at the local community college, along with exploring other options. She was able to narrow this down by going on college tours, apprentice interviews, and community college tours. **What was important was she was in search of a career no matter what qualifications were needed.** She was not focused on following the crowd. In an information session, she met a student who was studying in the dental hygienist program. She asked them all the questions she needed to know in order to make her decision. Along with observing her own dental experiences from the past.

She went in with a list of prepared questions. After chatting with her, I realized that any of us could use these while evaluating our career path options, regardless of what our interests are. Use these questions to help identify pros and cons for your specific industry/career choice.

1. How much does this program cost?
2. How long is the program?

3. Am I able to live on campus or at home during the program?
4. Is it reasonable to have a part-time job while in school?
5. What is the test for the certification?
6. How challenging is the test for the certification? What is the pass rate?
7. For the certification, do you have to do any sort of continuing education? If so, what are the requirements?
8. How many hours do you work a week, and what is your schedule like?
9. What does a typical day look like for you?
10. How far is your commute every day?
11. Do you have a mentor?
12. Do you need to have additional licenses to work in your field or to own your own business?
13. Are there different niches in the industry that I can go into? Do different niches provide a significant income increase?
14. Are there annual reviews in this field?
15. How did you know you liked this program and knew it was right for you?
16. How did you know this school was for you?
17. Did you find your place in society?
18. What are the benefits to having this job?
19. Are you able to cover your cost of living in society with the income you make?
20. What does your lifestyle budget look like? Do you eat out once a week? Are you saving after-tax dollars in an investment management account (brokerage account)?
21. What generations of people do you work with mainly?
22. Is the industry predominantly male or female?

23. What are the negatives to having this job?
24. What is this job *really* like?
25. How did you know you had a passion for this career?
26. How did you know something at this career fair *wasn't* for you?
27. How did you know something at this career fair *was* for you?
28. What is your uniform or dress code policy?
29. What is the hierarchy like in this industry?
30. Is there flexibility with the job/hours once I become a parent?
31. Do you get joy from helping people and being a productive member of society?
32. Do I have to travel a lot for this job?
33. What does the cost of living look like? What do pay increases look like throughout my career with promotions in this industry?
34. Do you have a hybrid or in-person policy?
35. Do you have a good work-life balance? (Meaning, you work and have the time and space to work out, go grocery shopping, go to dinner, etc. in your spare time without a lot of stress.)
36. What's the hard truth about this job?
37. Why do people like this career path?

ON-THE-JOB TIP: You can use some of these questions from this list for a job interview, too.

After asking these questions and many more, it really spoke to her that this career path was for her because it was attainable, something she was passionate about, and it fit the lifestyle that she wanted to have for her life.

The main selling points for her—aside from the cost of school—were that it was attainable and didn't require extensive test-taking.

She loved that she could work at a dentist's office where she would work ten hours four days a week. She'd be working four long days a week, spending each one with her hands in ten different mouths. She also loved the idea that she had a boss, but not someone who would micromanage her every move. Obviously, just like in school, her boss would oversee her work and come in after every cleaning and check on the patient's teeth cleaning. The dentist or owner gives feedback, but the dentist isn't over the dental hygienist's shoulders while she is actually cleaning. Dental hygienists have their own room to foster client relationships twice a year with their patients.

To top it off, if one of the Mondays was a federal holiday, she would get an even longer weekend because her day off was Tuesday. She could literally work another job waiting tables on the weekends if she wanted to while keeping all of the benefits at her full-time job during the week, or she could be working on that side hustle. She liked that if she had kids, she wouldn't have to pay for day care one day a week because she could be at home. It made the long days easier knowing she could turn the laundry over and be at home one day to do chores during the week while everyone else was at work. She loved the idea that she could have her own little morning routine and she could feel like she was on vacation every weekend.

While in school, she started as an administrative assistant at a dental office near her home, taking on the responsibilities of running the office. After graduating, she was promoted and now manages her own appointment office, where she also performs cleanings. She lived at home with her parents and began her planned budgeting strategy by "paying" herself rent, saving toward a down payment for a home.

She felt a sense of purpose, providing outstanding dental care to all different types of people who came in. She loved to talk, so it was a great job for her because it was a one-way conversation in most cases. After graduating high school at eighteen, she did the two-year program and passed the exam; she started making anywhere from $50,000 to $120,000 a year. She knew that this was enough money to sustain a lifestyle for herself while contributing to her 401(k) and paying for her own health insurance, starting at the age of twenty-six when she got off of her parents' plan. She knew it was her path to freedom of moving out because she was going to be able to cover the cost of living for her current and future self.

Figuring It Out as You Go

This exercise and process we just discussed is not easy, and it is not something that comes naturally to everyone. Something that you may not realize in high school or college is that your career will transition many times over; you will most likely not retire in the industry or at the company that you first started working at. That is okay and normal. You change, and your priorities change. Your motives for helping people and earning money change. As long as you stay connected to your network that you keep fostering, that's all that matters. Sometimes, the people you know can open doors that a diploma alone cannot. That's why you need to have pride in your name and all the work that you do.

Society welcomes you. As you are. You have something valuable to offer society. You are needed here—all of us are. Even if it sometimes feels like you're defined only by the stereotypes from grammar school, that's not who you truly are. You will see the big picture. Keep reminding yourself of the BIG picture! Sometimes it's easy to get lost in the small details of the day or things going on. It is awfully hard to see sometimes. Do not let others pass judgment on you or your goals. If they are passing judgment, that's because they are jealous you are focusing on you and figuring it out while they are wasting time judging you and not figuring out their own lives. Students lucky enough to get a four-year college education often feel like they have to figure out their career during those years spent in class. How on earth are all these adults making us decide what we want to do in society when we are still stuck in a classroom? Yes, we obviously have learned valuable things in a classroom that can be transferable to the real world. Yes, you have learned some things that are relevant to real life, even if you don't feel it. But getting out there and experiencing or shadowing careers can help you figure out your career path so you can cover your cost of living for yourself.

> ON-THE-JOB TIP: For adults reading this book, consider being a mentor to one person entering society. Help pull them up. Pick one person a year to help. Have them shadow you for one day. Post the opportunity on Facebook or your local newspaper. Society thanks you! The next generation thanks you. And we will pay it forward and do the same. A typical scientist in the field isn't one with a lab coat; there are so many different types of scientists, like a marine biologist scuba diving with sharks.

Next time you are driving around your town, write down all of the different businesses that operate there. Every town has pizza places, day cares, dance studios, a post office, electricians, internet providers, nail salons, car dealerships, and so on. Do your own research and figure out where you fit in so you can earn money to cover your cost of living. The only way you will be able to do this is to look at all—yes, *all*—the options. Knock one out every time it doesn't feel right. Feel free to go into a store and ask to shadow them for a day to see if you would like a career in the field. Society will respond and make you feel welcome.

Beyond that, ask your network what they do for a living. Next time you go to a family holiday party and the adults are interrogating you about what you are studying or how your summer job is going, start interrogating them. I DARE YOU. Ask them what their job is really like. Ask them how they figured out how to cover their cost of living and their families' cost of living; maybe do this in a way that doesn't directly ask them to share their salary. Ask them if they feel like they are making an impact on society.

Now, here's something to note: If you ask about their career and they are not passionate about it, it does NOT mean it is not for you. It just means it is not *for them*. Someone else might really like that job and feel fulfilled. (The same goes for college tours. Sometimes the tour guide might have had a long night or just isn't great at showing school spirit. That doesn't mean the school isn't right for you.)

You need to think of yourself as a business. You need to be able to cover your fixed costs each month with whatever you decide to do in life. It's hard because when you're high school or college age, you don't really know or understand what it will take to cover your costs as a person in society.

Your mandatory fixed costs include health insurance, 401(k)/retirement plan, groceries, toiletries, housing, car payment, self-care/gym memberships, clothes, cell phone plan, gas, etc.

Your variable costs include concert tickets, eating out, getting your nails done, optional technology, watches, purses, and basically anything that's not a necessity that fluctuates each month. This is where people live beyond their means and get in trouble. (See the Appendix on page 140 for personal balance sheets.)

Reaching out to your network can be really helpful, but it's also challenging—especially when you don't know what questions to ask. Think about your own experience: Did your parent figures start gradually shifting expenses to you when you got a job? Maybe you began by paying for gas, then car insurance, and eventually the car payments.

Use that as a model when talking to people in your network. Ask them practical questions like, "What does it take to run your household? How much does your home cost? What are typical expenses for self-care or weekend activities?" Remember, everyone's budget is different—and it changes at different stages of life.

As you grow, you will slowly start to realize what your budget is and what you can afford after all of your fixed costs are covered. This is when you ask your friends, parent figures, or other mentors in life what it takes for them to sustain their lifestyle.

Unfortunately, you won't be able to ask everybody these types of questions, and everybody will have different answers. Some people will have poor money-management skills and just say that they live paycheck to paycheck, budgeting different expenses every two weeks with whatever comes up; then you'll hear the complete opposite end of the spectrum, where people still live paycheck to paycheck, but they are also budgeting for their future self by saving in their 401(k)s or saving up to pay that car insurance.

I know this might be asking a lot considering you just started this book, but there are some other amazing books out there that talk about personal finance. Read some of the popular ones and take the tips you like and apply them to your lifestyle. (See Appendix II Book Recommendations on page 145 for a list of books that have impacted how I've found my own place in society; not all of the tips from these books will work for you, but some will be wildly helpful.)

My biggest recommendation is to have a planned budget, like we talked about earlier. At the bare minimum, contribute to your 401(k) at work as soon as possible and increase the contribution every year until you are maxing it out. If you are doing that, you are still ahead of the game. Also really do the research to find a career path that is right for you. Do not limit your options without looking into a career path to the fullest extent to be able to cross it off the list and say it's not for you. You can't say it isn't for you without seeing what it's like first.

Each person is destined for greatness and has a purpose in society. Each person has the right and freedom to cover their own cost of living. It's freeing to not rely on anyone but yourself. Being an adult means not being Frankie the Freeloader anymore.

KEY TAKEAWAYS:

- **Covering Your Cost.** Live below your means by living conservatively. It doesn't matter what you have materially; it matters what you have in the bank or assets that will get you to financial freedom.
- **Understand Retirement.** Retirement becomes possible when your other sources of income can fully replace your salary. Think of it this way: You're already practicing retirement every weekend—those are your days to do what you want. Use them intentionally. You've spent the week contributing to society; your time off is a preview of the freedom you're working toward.
- **Choosing a Career Wisely.** There's no one-size-fits-all path after high school. Whether it's trade school, community

college, a job, a gap year, or a traditional four-year college, the key is to explore options that align with your interests and strengths. The goal isn't just to land a job—it's to gain skills, experience, and the confidence to build a meaningful career over time.

CHAPTER 4

LEARNING HOW TO EARN

Until now, you've been carried by a system—structured classes, assigned homework, and scheduled tests. But things are changing. You're stepping into a world where *you* are responsible for planning your life, managing money, and finding purpose. The biggest shift is that you start earning instead of learning for a living.

For years, you've followed a set curriculum, absorbing knowledge and moving to the next step. But the real world rewards *active* learning—asking questions, seeking out answers, and staying curious. You'll need to get comfortable asking, "I don't know—can you help me understand?" Asking questions doesn't make you weak; it makes you smart. And yes, people actually think you're smart when you ask good questions.

Think back on your teachers. The great ones made an impact. The less great ones? Maybe you blamed them when you didn't understand something. But here's the hard truth: In the working world, you can't blame the boss for your confusion. You have to ask questions, seek feedback, and own your learning. That mindset starts now.

And while school might not have taught you to be an independent thinker, *life* will. Not all responsibility falls on teachers—your circle of influence matters. Who you learn from and surround yourself with will shape you just as much.

Eventually, it's on *you* to decide what you want to do with your life and how you want to contribute. That responsibility can feel overwhelming. One moment you're in high school, the next you're part of society.

Embracing the Unknown and Starting the Journey

Stepping into adulthood can feel like crossing an invisible line—suddenly, the world is wide open, and the possibilities are endless. It's exciting, but also overwhelming. You're no longer just a student in a familiar system—you're part of a much bigger world. Do not get gobbled up by society. You are destined for greatness. Remember to always think of this as a positive opportunity. Do not let the opening of society cripple you with anxiety. Even though it may feel like it for a second. Just know that you don't have to reinvent the wheel here. You don't need to figure out a career path that's unknown. You just need to be yourself and enjoy what you do.

Take me for example. Did I actually think that this world needed another self-help book? YES! Because what I had to say and the spin I wanted to put on it matters. I am convinced this is a brand. Was I writing this book on nights and weekends when I wasn't in my nine-to-five? YES! Learn from everyone before you, and use your resources around you. Start asking the questions and driving the conversations to create your own path in society.

When I started looking for my first job, I leaned on the resources around me—career services, LinkedIn, and job search sites—to find internships and opportunities. To be completely honest, my résumé was full of fun sports or activities I did in high school. I had no real experience. You will likely apply for jobs in the future that you are not qualified for, but you will need to find creative ways to stand out. The way I marketed myself was that I can hustle and manage having multiple things going on at once and be efficient with them all. You don't need much to get creative with how you present yourself in an interview. Some tips for landing a job include the following:

- Provide a list of examples similar to a project they are hiring for.
- Keep following up, and write thank-you letters.
- If you've applied more than once to the same place, show how you've grown.
- Tell your network you are looking for a job and that you'd appreciate any leads.

This takes practice—you're doing it for the first time and taking the leap into the working world. Remember there is a profession called *recruiting*, and a recruiter's job is to help place professionals in society. It is a full-time job finding a job. It's exhausting. I realized if I wanted to be an entrepreneur, I needed to start small with different changes. I needed to watch shows like *Shark Tank* and not reality TV. I needed to surround myself with like-minded people. I didn't want to be the smartest person in the room or make myself feel better by watching reality stars mess up their lives. The question that I kept asking myself was, *What is universal, like a birthday, that everyone goes through in life, and how can I make money fixing this problem?* That's why adults are all jealous of you . . . because you are young and have time to do this.

> ON-THE-JOB TIP: Interviewing is a skill. If you are interviewing for a few jobs, and there is one out of the bunch that you really want, book that interview last out of the bunch so you get practice at the other interviews.

Eventually, you'll walk into a room where you feel seen, welcomed, and like you truly belong. If you haven't felt that, then you aren't where you are supposed to be. Keep exploring ways to grow and find new opportunities; try different things and meet different people—one day, you'll find your place.

How Did You Learn to Earn?

One thing that often goes unsaid is the importance of learning how to earn money—and understanding the different ways that's possible. I think we can talk about money without talking about how much money you have. We can ask people—your family, your friends, parent figures, your teachers, and your mentors—how they learned to earn money.

Think about that question just for yourself: How did you learn to earn money? You've probably learned to earn money because your parent figures told you now that you can drive, you need to pay for gas and maybe the car insurance in high school when you first got your license. Or maybe you got a swifter kick in the you-know-what. "You want a lifestyle, college, gas, car . . . Well, you're old enough to go to work, so get to it." You went to work at a local restaurant or the local grocery store so you could earn gas money to drive yourself to practice, school, games, and work. Good job, you, and good job, parent figures.

That answers my question, right? Sort of. Other than getting told you're old enough to start working, how did you *learn to earn* money?

Did you learn how to earn money at a lemonade stand in your town? Did you do the hard work of making the lemonade and lemonade sign, then dragging it out to the street corner with a huge smile and trying to wave down customers? Did you learn the hard truths about business and watch some cars just drive by without even honking and buying a glass from your cute face? The nerve. They taught you a powerful lesson in business, though. Not everyone is a customer. Not everyone will buy what you're selling. Failing is good. Rejection is good, even though it just completely stinks in the moment. Make sure it only lasts a moment!

It's a loaded question: How did you learn to earn money? Because you just read *Macbeth* in English, and you just did an introduction to chemistry course, but did you learn how to earn money? You learned what you liked and what you didn't like, which is very helpful. You will either be an employee or own your own business in your lifetime, and the one critical question that you should ask your community of people that are on your bus is, *How did you learn to earn your money?*

What's beautiful is that the answers will all be different. That's what makes us all destined for greatness and to impact society in a positive way. **The greatest answer to this question that I've heard is, "I did what I loved, and the money came second."** That's a very woo-woo answer, but it is also true! They found what they loved after trial and error. Yes, trial and error. You will not graduate and go into a career path that you will likely stay in your entire career. That's just not realistic. That's okay; you didn't know you wouldn't like that lifestyle or career path until you got a taste of it. There is NO PRESSURE to get it right the first time. Yes, life is precious, but you have plenty of time to figure it out and grow your network in the process.

Some people say their mother was very creative and artsy while they were growing up. They enjoyed their marketing classes in college and then started working for a company. Over time, by fostering relationships and earning people's trust year after year—while those clients relied on their creativity to drive higher sales—they eventually opened their own marketing firm. Like, wow! But that paragraph of professional events took ten to twenty years of learning on the job after being a student for twenty years.

Some will simply say, "My dad was a dentist and owned his own dental practice, and if I followed in his footsteps, I could own that office one day." Yes, some people might think that's a nepo baby, but I also believe that they would be crazy not to take that opportunity to walk into an established business. One day, they can call it their own after working with their family every day. Working with family is amazing because whoever you are working with, you are spending the majority of your time with during the week, so if you get along with your family, join your family business. But, if you try it and it's not for you, that's good to know as well.

Some people are cringing at the idea of their mom or dad being their boss or coworker. It would just be a continuation of childhood, some would say. Others would treasure spending that much time with their parent figures and witnessing how respected and admired they are in society. Others will rebel and do the complete opposite of whatever their family is interested in or field they work in. It's all good.

Some drive a hard bargain and are very bottom-line focused; they say they learned how to earn in a way where it doesn't matter how much they bill in their business. It matters how much they collect and put in their pocket.

You can bill whatever you want (whatever someone is willing to pay for your services), but if you don't cash that check, then you didn't earn the money if collectibles are out there.

You see what we are doing here? Bringing in covering your cost of living and money management into learning how to earn! Sounds familiar, right? You have to run yourself like a business when it comes to your income and budgeting to cover your cost of living. The same goes for how much money goes into your bank account within each pay period if you are an employee and don't own your own business.

Do you know how much of the money you earn actually stays with you as you build your net worth or save for future opportunities? Making $1 million a year sounds impressive, but if your fixed costs are equally high and you spend it all, how wealthy are you really? How wealthy do you appear to others? And ultimately, does it matter if people are watching how much money you have?

They will probably never be able to guess how much money you actually have saved up in the bank until you're the one who's retired and living with financial freedom at the age of sixty or even fifty years old.

Look at some of the wealthiest people in America; they are still working just for the social aspect, and they genuinely like what they do. However, it's also possible they have big lifestyles they still need to afford and pay for.

Take this question on how you learn to earn money and ask everyone what their answer is. I think you will be amazed at what people share. How do we take that question and make it a part of the curriculum when you're a student? I don't know if I have the answer to that. You can learn about different careers on career days, but you probably won't truly find your answer until you start doing what you love—letting the money come second. It's only by making connections between what you learn in the classroom and the realities of the working world that you'll begin to understand your path.

Society knows you are young, dumb, and broke, and society knows that life gets harder; it's a balancing act. The greatest thing that you can do to keep humbling yourself is to remember your fundamental needs: shelter, water, and income. Everything else in life that you accomplish is extra and amazing. We are all destined for greatness. It is no one else's responsibility to help you get from student to society other than yourself. Don't play the blame game. You don't deserve anything. UGH! I know the eye roll. I felt it! But it's true. You will earn everything you have in life and have a lot of pride in it.

So, how did you learn to earn money? When did you start earning money? Did you babysit, work in food and beverage service, or bag groceries? Or did you start before that?

My guess is you might've been in the lunchroom when you were negotiating chips for candy bars simply because you wanted some candy at lunch. Or maybe you went to camp and received an allowance for the camp store—and you realized you could buy items there and resell them at a higher price to other kids who didn't have an allowance. You were resourceful. You learned about supply and demand on your own. You learned the value of maintaining relationships.

Let's look at some people's answers for how they learned to earn.

> "It was never about what someone could do for you in the short term. It was always about what we could do for each other over the long haul. I have always been in the business of long-term relationships. Let's go through the highs and the lows together. Sharing our experiences at different points in life builds trust in one another and shows that our

incomes matter—not just for ourselves, but to support each other and our families. Those long-term relationships in life were never taken for granted. We were always reasonable with each other."
—*Aerospace logistics manager, thirty years old*

"It's what you make it. If you get frustrated by the littlest thing and say you want to quit, that will most likely be your attitude if you were to go to a different company, too. Nothing is perfect."
—*Electrical lineman, thirty years old*

"One skill is just learning how to work with others. It seems as though in school there is one group project for every class every semester, and it is always a fight to get to the finish line, but you will be working on teams when you enter the real world. In those class group projects, there always seemed to be one student that wouldn't hold their own weight because they knew the rest of the team would carry them through the semester project. Learn how to deal with every type of person. What motivates them? How did you deal with teammates on the field if they had a bad day? This is all relatable and transferable to working with difficult people in the real world. Those difficult people in the real world are most likely your well-paying customers, though. A good manager can manage anyone. So start practicing now. Didn't you see your parent figures raise you and your siblings differently? They had to manage you all differently because you would all respond in different ways to different approaches. Learn this skill as early as possible. Do what you need to do or say to get what you want out of the situation in the first place."

—Customer account relations representative, forty years old

When I've taught college-level courses, I allowed the group to fire team members who weren't contributing. I only allowed them to fire the team member after they went through the different HR protocols that you see in the real world, however. First, there's usually a verbal warning; second, there's usually a written warning; and the third warning usually means you're out. Just like the consequences that we talked about in the connecting student to society chapter.

ON-THE-JOB TIP: You might be surprised, but a moment like this could actually be a great example to use in a job interview. In many interviews I've been in, one question that always comes up is, *"How do you handle stress or conflict?"* It's a powerful question because it reveals a lot about your character. That's why it's so important to have a thoughtful answer—ideally a real story that demonstrates your ability to stay calm, show emotional maturity, and maintain a positive attitude as part of a team. Make sure your answers aren't just surface-level. Share full, honest stories that show who you are and how you work with others under pressure.

Small activities like that actually reflect real-world situations and are important to understand while you're still in school. However, teachers often don't have the time to focus on those aspects—or they're so focused on teaching the core principles of a group project that real-world job expectations get left out. Little principles like that would be so helpful to learn younger so when you are in society, you are prepared for how things operate in business.

> "Learning how to earn is all about understanding the hierarchy in a business and realizing you can climb it. Understanding that there are the students at the bottom of the barrel; above them are the teachers and custodial workers and the lunchroom ladies; then above them is the principal; then above them are the superintendent and the school committee; and then above them is the teacher's union or state committees for teacher associations. That whole hierarchy is built off of people that have been in the place before and have worked their way up the pole. Realizing that you were at the bottom of the barrel is freeing and humbling. You have no say, and you have to respect everyone, but also just respect the hierarchy. There will be a hierarchy at whatever company you work at, and you will have to respect that. You don't necessarily have to respect them as a person if they are a bad egg, but you have to respect their title. If you understand the hierarchy, you will understand how to earn more money. Whether that be through certifications, years in a career, getting mentored by the right people, etc."
> *—College professor, fifty years old*

> "The answer to this is obviously balance. You have the responsibility to wake up early in the morning and go to work and be a productive human in society now. Not that you weren't a productive human in society when you were studying, but there's more on the line here because

you could lose all you've worked hard for just because you weren't productive throughout the day at work. Some people have this 'work hard, play hard' mentality, and if you had that in school where you partied every Thursday, Friday, and Saturday night, but during the day you ordered a large coffee and went to the library, then that's great. You were still getting your work done; the same thing applies for when you have the typical nine-to-five job. You're getting old. You won't be able to burn the candle at both ends for long. You will complain about being tired as you juggle life just like the rest of us."
—Real estate agent, thirty years old

"Not being a know-it-all! Being uncomfortable with not knowing everything but having the confidence to know you can figure it out or network and connect with someone who does will make you rich! There is no possible way you know everything, whether you want to admit it or not. HELLO! That's why everyone specializes in something different. There's no way I could know how to do both brain surgery and do electrical work at an expert level. So that same feeling you have in the classroom when the teacher says, 'Any questions?' and you were thinking about butterflies or cars. Know you will feel like that in adulthood. One thing to keep in mind is that we are all always learning, and we can all always learn from each other. It was humbling to realize this at the beginning of my career. Have you ever realized that a doctor doesn't say they're a doctor? They say that they are 'practicing medicine.' Have you ever realized

that a CPA sometimes doesn't say they're an actual CPA, but they say they are a 'practicing tax accountant'? I think it humbles the professional to a human level when they say they are practicing whatever brings them joy and is their job because they are always learning and practicing on the job!"
—Secretary, seventy years old

"Everyone needs to know sales to some capacity. Sales is the groundwork for all forms of business. You need to be able to sell yourself in an interview with your elevator pitch to get a job or change jobs. You need to have and grow tough skin. You need to learn how to take denial."
—Medical device sales manager, forty years old

"This may be more of a life skill or a rite of passage, but what has helped me learn how to earn is to understand the difference between when you can control something and when you have no control over something. In life and your career, there will be a lot you can control, but there will be a lot that you can't control. Knowing the difference is important and crucial for those instances when you have no control and you need to be brave in order to 'bounce back' as fast as possible."
—Restaurateur, sixty years old

"Be you. You will pull the good people toward you if you are a good person. You will have positive relationships with others if you are positive. Be the person you wish to be surrounded by, and you will be propelled further in life."
—Veterinary hospital clerk, thirty years old

"One of the first things that I was told and given advice on when I started my first internship was to befriend the administrative assistants. They know all the gossip in the office. They know you are an intern. I'm here to tell you that they probably have some weight on the decision of you in the office. They will also go out of their way to help you if you address them and offer to get them a coffee once in a while. They know all the gossip in the office, so don't overshare with them either. They are the moms at the office. Lean on them like that."
—*Wealth management intern, twenty years old*

"Be nice to everyone. I was behind someone at the grocery store who was giving the high school student cashier a hard time. When they walked away, I told them they handled it well and with class. The bagger goes, 'Don't worry. I took care of her and put her bread and chips at the bottom of the bags.' I cried laughing. That's called karma in the streets."
—*Salon owner, forty years old*

"I want to make a really important differentiation. I want to highlight the difference between being likable and wanting to be liked by people who want to fit in. There is a universal want and need to fit in with society. There is a universal want and need to be likable in order to do business or to earn an income. There is a universal want or need to be cool. I think there are some things that we can learn, and I think these younger generations are already starting to pinpoint them, which is that being cool is being who you are meant to be.

We gravitate toward people who are authentic online. We can be those authentic people in our communities or at school. We can be inclusive. Being likable in business only gets you more business, which equals more money."
—*Marketing design manager, thirty years old*

"The most important lessons in learning how to earn usually come down to two things: doing right by people and having solid business ethics. For example, if you refer a client of yours to someone else for a consultation or extra work beyond your scope, you would expect that the referral business would not permanently take your client going forward. If they do, they are stealing your money, income, clients, hard work, and relationships. Yes, all's fair in love and war. But we should never be so greedy as to take someone else's business so foolishly like that. As big as this world is, the PR of bad business spreads quickly. Haven't you seen people on your town's Facebook page call out a contractor or business that treated them poorly—warning others not to hire them? This ties directly into earning and doing right by others. If you genuinely enjoy what you do and care about helping people, you'll naturally treat them well—even if they've wronged you—because how you handle those moments reflects your character and professionalism. It's sort of like the woes of dealing with your parent figures and in-laws in contentious conversations about wedding planning. It is the first time you are doing a group project with your parent figures, and it completely messes with you! You will still see your in-laws after the

> wedding, just like you will see the client around your town or in business in the future. You need to be able to say you held your head up high on the way out of a bad conversation and be proud of how you handled it. Doing right by people only earns you more referrals or more money. But, ultimately, it should earn you a sense of pride that you can go to sleep knowing you did the right thing."
>
> —*HVAC business owner, thirty years old*

I want to elaborate on being likable in business. In school, a transferable skill that you can bring from school to the real world is being likable and being friends with everybody. You can never have enough friends in business. If you're heading off to college or another advanced education program, I hope you go out every weekend—because whether you realize it or not, you're actually networking. You are networking with the people who will be in your life and in your early professional career. Everyone in your mandatory senior business class is likely applying for the same jobs as you—and you'll probably run into them again at networking events during your first few years after graduation. You need to remember that there's a difference between being likable in business and going through your life pleasing people.

On the job, there will be people that are not well liked. Can you think of the one person that is typically not liked in an office? The boss. It doesn't matter if they're super cool and nice; they are still the boss. Be that person in the office who gets along with everyone. If you are the only person who can get along with so-and-so, then you are creating job security for yourself because you will likely be partnered with them to help the team accomplish the monthly goal.

You want to be known as the person who can work with anyone. It's very marketable for you.

Is there still a desire to be the most popular person in school or the prettiest or the most athletic? Yes. I think those social norms will always sort of stick around to some capacity. Social norms sometimes define you in your community, and that's okay. You will gravitate toward your people.

You're in the right group because you're surrounded by like-minded people. Find your people—and take comfort in knowing that they're yours for a reason.

Don't try to climb the social ladder, because you'll probably be trying for the rest of your life. There are parent figures or adults in my town who are trying to be the coolest, and they are looking for that external satisfaction. They are the materialistic ones who are not saving money and trying to buy friends. If that makes them happy, then that's okay. Just know you don't have to keep up with the Joneses. The grass isn't always greener on the other side. Just mind your own grass.

In this one precious life, find the courage and the subtle confidence to try new things. You don't know what you don't know until you've tried it and really sit back and evaluate and think about how it feels. Does it make you happy to do these new things, or was that new thing just not for you? It's completely okay if it's not for you; just move on, bury it in your brain, and try the next thing.

One thing that you learn when you become a parent is that you cannot compare your child to other children. Because each child that is blessed to be on this earth is destined for greatness in their own way and in their own capacity. Each child will find the people they're meant to fit in with. We will all surround ourselves with people who love us for who we are and won't try to change us.

Learning to earn is an everyday example in life. The more life experience you have, the more you will be able to apply it to your professional life.

KEY TAKEAWAYS

- **Teachers Spark the Start—But You Own the Journey.** Teachers often serve as your first mentors, guiding you into society by teaching both academic content and life skills. But as you grow, your progress depends on your willingness to take responsibility for your learning—both in and out of the classroom.
- **Growth Comes from Doing What's New.** Applying for jobs, writing a résumé, and figuring out your career path can feel overwhelming—but that's normal. Like any new skill, the process gets easier with practice. Start small, trust yourself, and allow space to grow through the experience.
- **Learning to Earn Happens Everywhere.** Earning money isn't something most people are formally taught. Instead, we pick it up through life experience, advice from others, and trial and error. Whether it's book smarts or street smarts, what matters is your ability to adapt, observe, and take action.

CHAPTER 5

GETTING TO KNOW YOURSELF (NO PRESSURE)

Before we dive any deeper and risk overwhelming you with things you may have never considered, take a moment. Hopefully, everything you've just read has sparked some reflection about who you are—and where you're headed. There's no class on this in school. It's all introspective thinking and brainstorming.

Let's take a step back and see how far you have come. Let's gain some confidence back after feeling like we were in a tornado. Let's reflect in order to move forward with your future.

Now, with too much reflection, you could feel like you haven't even moved anywhere. You may even feel like your progress is pulling you backward. It's like a sinking feeling—day in and day out. Working toward a goal or career but not feeling that momentum like you are progressing. Maybe it's because you aren't getting regular grades anymore that are satisfying.

I call this the slingshot theory.

The Slingshot Theory: Trust the Process

It's normal to be pulled back in life and have setbacks: Maybe you are changing jobs, living with your parent figures, deciding to go to law school, or changing careers, etc. You get pulled backward, and that sinking feeling creeps in—that maybe you'll never move forward in life. But then, like releasing a slingshot, everything launches ahead so quickly it almost feels unreal. Everything that you have been working toward starts happening. Suddenly you have moved into your own home after saving while at your parents' house, back in the industry where you belong after being the new kid again at work, or you graduate law school. Life will happen quickly, and all that hard work will pay off. It just comes quicker (so enjoy it) than the hard work to get there.

I had the hardest time writing this chapter, which is weird and completely embarrassing to admit, considering I'm talking about people understanding themselves. I should know this chapter so well. I should know myself so well.

It feels like there is such a hard deadline on knowing all of these things, but especially for knowing yourself and what you want to do and who you want to be in society. The reality is there is no deadline. So take a deep breath and get that monkey off your back.

No Deadline for Knowing Yourself

The transition into society can feel overwhelming, but it's just one of the many transitions in life. Everyone connects with themselves in different ways—whether it's hiking, journaling, or meditation. These practices help clear out the noise so you can focus on your mind, body, and spirit. There's no one-size-fits-all method, so take the time to figure out what works for you. When you understand yourself, you can show up for society with your best foot forward, and your relationships will improve as a result.

Some say the greatest gift is growing in life and learning about yourself. I was told college would be the best years of my life, a time when I would learn *everything* about myself—but the reality is it's just one chapter in a long journey. As life moves forward, you'll notice how society scatters after school—your friends will be in different towns, and you'll realize your network is expanding across the country, even globally. This is part of the beauty of life.

You're either earning or learning, as my mother always said. If you have the opportunity to educate yourself, take it. But remember, the goal is to keep growing beyond school—don't peak there.

When we were babies, we instinctively knew what we didn't want, like turning our faces from peas. Similarly, don't let society force things on you that don't feel right. Trust your instincts and follow through on what you truly want. That's the real trick—pursue your own dreams, not what others expect of you.

At some point in college or in your twenties, you'll realize that you need to be your own pillar of stability. You're no longer relying on others—parent figures, partners, or anyone else—and you will need to build your own foundation and financial independence. You need to only rely on yourself. This is part of the journey of growing into who you are meant to be. I have a love-hate relationship with the word *journey*. It's a great word, but it's wildly overused. *Trip*, *expedition*, *passage*, and *ride* also just don't cut it.

Take Care of You: Show Up for Yourself First

Another thing worth mentioning about self that is completely underrated is self-love when it comes to grooming yourself. Remember that fifth-grade talk from the teacher? "You don't want to be the stinky kid." Remember when everyone was going through puberty, and the teacher would sit the class down to talk about hygiene? They'd say, "No one wants to be the stinky kid." You definitely didn't want to be known as the smelly one in your grade. You got told you should wear deodorant and start showering once a day. I'm sure we all probably thought that the teacher was talking about us or knew the student she was referencing.

The same still applies whether you like it or not. It's really important to shower and do your hair every day—and maybe even wear a little makeup—to show up as your best self each day. Do you ever watch those rom-coms in which the woman gets ready for an hour just to go to the grocery store? That holds true because you never know who you're going to meet. Didn't Tyra Banks get her start in modeling from her passport photo? I know what you're thinking: *I'm no Tyra Banks; I'm no supermodel.* Neither am I, so don't worry. It's always important to put your best self forward. It's just good to make yourself feel good and authentic to who you want to show to society.

So don't be the smelly kid: Get up and shower, brush your teeth, floss twice a day, brush your hair, make sure your nails are painted, and put on your best shoes. Because looking good and starting your day with a solid morning or night routine can make a real difference in your confidence—and even in your career. If you have a presentation at school, don't you still pick out an outfit—kind of like your first-day-of-school outfit—that just makes you feel good and ready to take on the day? Yeah. We all do. If you look good, you feel good. Continue to wear your favorite work outfit to big presentation days, or even go out and spend a few bucks on a new outfit. This is a transferable habit into society that "adults" do at their jobs, too. I had a huge presentation at my internship one year, and my assigned mentor—which is different from the mentor you want to emulate—actually gave me some great advice and said to go out and buy a new outfit I would feel good in so I would perform well. I know I'm *smart*, but the clothes really did help with my confidence. I obviously nailed the presentation—and I'll never forget the mentor in the audience giving me two enthusiastic thumbs-ups. If you really want to know, I did not get a full-time offer to go back after graduation, even though I did way better than some of the other students at that presentation. Whether you believe me now or not, there are many things you do now in school that have prepared you for the real world.

ON-THE-JOB TIP: Keep a toiletry bag in your desk (deodorant, mints, hand sanitizer, etc.). You may need to brush your teeth after lunch before a big meeting.

Morning and night routines are buzzwords in the adult world these days—and if you ask the most successful people out there, they'll each point to their own unique routine as a key part of what makes them successful. If you are allotting a lot of time throughout your day for clients, patients, family members, and your dog, you should obviously (but it's not so obvious sometimes) take time for yourself and have a little "me" time. Personally, my favorite me-time activity is to ride the couch and watch trash TV; after a long day of using my brain, I want to watch people that don't use their brains. They are the ones flying private, and I'm riding the couch. (Maybe they do use their brains?)

You are what you consume, so I realized I could become a Real Housewife unless I start to focus on a more productive five-to-nine hobby.

In the adult world, there's not much "me" time, so you have to carve it out either in the morning or at night to either set yourself up for a day of success or to wind yourself down from the day. This time is so sacred; this time is fundamental to your well-being and how you show up for yourself and for society. Everyone has a different routine that they think makes them successful, whether it's the green juice in the morning or the early morning workout or the late-night reading time before bed.

Just a side note, if an influencer drinks thirty ounces of celery juice every day to make themselves feel good, that doesn't necessarily mean that's what you should do. Trust me…green juice is yucky. You ultimately need to listen to your body and mind to figure out a routine that works for you. You can use what their routines are as a guide. You should cherry-pick what you like and don't like after trying it for a while.

Regardless of what you explore, as long as you are consistent about showing up for yourself a little bit each day, then that's really all you need. Committing yourself is a virtue. It's not so much about *what* you do during that time—it's about *making* the time. Taking even a few selfish minutes for yourself is powerful. That's when you really connect with who you are and what you need.

Consistency Is Key

You also want to be known for being really consistent; if you can show up for yourself, people will know that you consistently will show up for them and your work. It connects back to being your own pillar of strength.

Figuring yourself out is like creating your own personal society. The more you understand your personality, strengths, and weaknesses, the more you can show up fully—in your community, your friendships, and your family.

Another final key to having a strong sense of self is not talking badly to yourself or listening to the negative thoughts in your brain. Being mean to yourself doesn't soften the blow for when someone is mean to you. Don't be your own bully. You are what you think. If you think you're awesome, then you are, in fact, awesome. Don't let people bring you down. If you do, and you lose yourself for a minute, you are entitled to a short five-minute pity party for yourself. But then, train your brain and say nice things to yourself again. Be your own superman or superwoman in your dreams who saves you from the nightmares. No one else will do this for you—and you should especially not put that pressure on your loved ones, specifically family.

> **ON-THE-JOB TIP:** Be the positive one in the office. People gravitate to it.

KEY TAKEAWAYS

- **Being You Is the Best Thing You Can Do.** Your unique personality, interests, and dreams are your greatest assets. Embrace the slingshot theory: When you work hard and stay consistent, even small efforts will launch you forward. Trust the process—there's no rush, and there's no deadline for becoming your best self.
- **Show Up for Yourself First.** Whether it's putting on deodorant or taking a moment to reset, taking care of yourself

is step one. You can't show up for school, work, or others if you're not showing up for *you*. Self-care isn't selfish—it's foundational.

- **Consistency Is Power.** You don't have to go full speed every day. Progress is built in the small, steady steps. Even when motivation is low, showing up and putting in a little effort makes a big impact over time.

CHAPTER 6

FAMILY: YOUR FIRST LESSON IN SOCIETY

Your society grew from you to your family.

Let's start small and work our way to society as we know it. We typically start life as part of someone else's dream. Often it was our parent figures' dream to have a family or child of their own. Even if that is not how it started for you, one thing is for certain: We are all here for a purpose. We are all here to make a difference in society. We are loved and raised by a traditional or nontraditional family.

No matter how you started, there are people in your early childhood who have influenced who you are today. Regardless of your influences, background, and socioeconomic status, YOU are destined for greatness. You do *belong* in society. Remember: YOU ARE DESTINED FOR GREATNESS regardless of who your family is.

There comes a point when you start focusing on—or consciously choose to build—your own stability. It's a shift from relying on others to creating a foundation you can stand on, one step at a time. Maybe you grew up in a loving home and learned how to create that stability for yourself from your family that mirrored it, or maybe you were the best friend to someone in a stable family, and you were the honorary extra sibling and learned about routines, stability, and kindness from them. Or maybe you came from a broken home, and the uncertainty and flexibility that were learned over the years led you to create a strong core within yourself in spite of that.

You learn values and life lessons from the people around you. Even as the youngest with older siblings, you observed their choices—both good and bad—and used those experiences to make even wiser decisions for yourself. (To my younger brothers: You're welcome.)

Your First Society

All families are different. All parent figures are different. Everyone's experiences are different. That's what makes society and your family beautiful. Your family is your first introduction to society beyond yourself. Consider them your first bubble.

Maybe you watched one parent stay at home and take care of the house while your other parent went to work at five a.m. Or you grew up with a bunch of friends that were your family in a foster home. Maybe you have two moms, and one worked nights and one worked days, so you were with one of them at all time! Perhaps your grandmother raised you all on her own. The combinations are endless. That first bubble of people that was around you was your first introduction to society.

Take the time to think back and see how your family operated. Who made the money and covered the cost of living? What traditions did you have, and what routines did your family follow growing up? Were birthdays or holidays special? Who taught you to brush your teeth? Who brushed your teeth before you knew what a toothbrush was? Did you have the infamous family meetings growing up from your parent figures about some sort of lesson or thing that you did wrong? Did you actually listen to them? Probably not. Can you think of them now? Were you in a dictatorship with one parent ruling the roost, making all the decisions and/or doing everything for you?

Did your parent figures work while you were in school, leaving you to get home on your own and do whatever you wanted until they returned? Have you ever thought that the way they raised you is because they were raised that way, or they were raised the complete opposite way and wanted to do everything differently?

Ask your parent figures these questions. Ask how they wanted to raise you to be a productive member of society. That's the hardest job they have; they have to raise you to be independent to be able to live without them.

Your parent figures have been where you have been before; your grandparents have been where your parent figures have been before—hierarchy strikes again! We can all learn from our experiences to be a great member of society regardless of our upbringings. Sounds familiar, right? Hierarchy and respect for the people before you. This is where you learned it and transferred it to the working world. Remember we talked about this—even though you don't like your boss, you have to respect them because they have been where you are before.

As you grow into adulthood, the dynamic with your family begins to shift. What once felt like a power struggle may actually just be guidance. The moment you realize that your parent figures or guardians aren't trying to control you but are offering advice based on their own experiences or mistakes, it can change everything. Try not to stay on the defensive. Most of the time, they're not criticizing; they're cheering you on as they watch you grow.

I will spare you the embarrassment and family meeting: Please *do not* tell your parent figures that you are an adult until you are paying for your own rent, groceries, toilet paper, health insurance, phone bill, clothes, vacations, and more. Because until you are, you are just Frankie the Freeloader.

What officially defines you as an independent adult in society functioning outside of your family unit? When do you get the freedom away from your parent figures? Is it when you can start to drive? Are you an adult when you start getting a paycheck? Is it when you turn eighteen and you can buy lottery tickets and vote? Or how about when you turn twenty-one and are legally able to buy liquor? Are you an adult when you start to like coffee or have a baby? Are you an adult when you cover your own health insurance at twenty-six? Are you an adult when you can cover your cost of living?

Does age matter, or is it a matter of maturity, responsibility, and emotional intelligence?

Before you give your parent figures any attitude about not emptying the dishwasher, just take a deep breath, be grateful, and empty the dishwasher. In reality, the dishwasher chore is small compared to having the responsibility of going to work every day to pay for the family's expenses.

Your family is shaped with different people that operate differently. We all know or have the slacker middle brother, or the uptight older sister, or the overly engaged parent figure who has no boundaries. Take a step back and think about your family's traits as a whole and individually. What do you observe?

At the end of the day, your chosen family or closest inner circle that you call family is very important. It is paramount to show up for your family in good times and in bad times. That's what family does.

Showing Up for Family

Do you want to be known as the person who is always there for someone? Do you want to be known as the fun family member, the most reliable, or the most stable? Probably all three. How do you want to be known within your family? For me, I want to be known as the laughing, kind, stable, loyal, and fun member of my family, classroom, and society. **We can make an impact on other students, society, and family members every day. I rise. You rise. We all rise.**

That first introduction into society in the walls of the house you grew up in shaped how you view the world and what you thought was normal. Then you met friends at school and went to their houses for playdates and met their families' norms. Were these norms different? Did they work better for you? Did you ever go home to Mom or Dad and tell them how Susie's mom did something that you liked better? Probably. Did you hurt your mom's feelings? Probably.

My brother once went over to the neighbor's house to have dinner with them, and he came home and told my mom that the dinner was so good. Out of curiosity, my mom texted the neighbor and asked her what was for dinner, and the neighbor told her it was grilled chicken and rice pilaf. She laughed because that is such a simple dinner, but he loved rice pilaf, so my mom started making it at least once a week.

As you get older, you start to realize everything that your parent figures have done to give you the childhood that you had. We all know that our childhood does not determine our outcome in life. When you sit down and think about your childhood, regardless of the ups and downs or so-called childhood traumas, the fact is the majority of us had the essentials: shelter, food, and an education.

You are probably at the age right now that you are starting to build your own life. You are so busy, and your mom isn't ruling the calendar anymore. Yes, hopefully you are starting to book your own doctor and dentist appointments annually (life-skill alert). News flash: You will be booking these appointments for your own kids soon.

Yes, it's hard for your parent figures to suddenly not know exactly what you're doing every day—especially when it feels like just yesterday they were organizing your entire schedule with school events, birthday parties, and sports games. You are probably at the age right now that your entire family is so busy that your parent figures have to book a vacation to get everyone in the same room and to also make memories for that team of people. Whatever the case may be, all of your upbringings are entangled with blessings and lessons.

It is probably hitting your parent figures very hard that the family they've created over the years will now start to branch off and create their own families, so let your parent figures treasure every ounce of time that they have left, and don't take the time that you're spending with them for granted. Remember that your parent figures won't be on this earth forever. They will remind you how they took care of you for years and that it is your turn to take care of them soon.

Preparing for Life's Uncertainties

One of the first times I really felt the weight of growing up was when I realized my parents wouldn't always be around. It hit during a swirl of college talk, looming responsibilities, and the quiet stress of being the oldest sibling. I wanted to stay a kid—go to track practice, laugh with friends—but the idea of adulthood started creeping in. Around the same time, I got my license, and with that came this big wave of independence. Suddenly, I didn't need my parents to pick me up from school—I could get myself home for dinner. It felt freeing until real responsibility showed up, like my first car accident—total panic, trying to remember everything from health class and adulthood prep. You realize fast that your actions are yours alone now. That independence, while exciting, also made things like the "if anything happens to us" talk from my parents feel way too real. It wasn't just a hypothetical—it was a reminder that life could change in an instant. But even in that realization, I found a deeper appreciation for what my parents did for us and a lot of gratitude for the times we're all still together, especially on the holidays.

Obviously, my parents always assured me that everything was handled and that all I had to worry about was being a kid. Come to find out, years later, my parents had an estate plan set up with a guardianship put in place where a family member would have taken care of us since we were under the age of eighteen.

Thoughtful, well-established families and adults usually have a plan like this in place. Being sophisticated and having an estate plan is important. Not saying my parents were wildly rich, but they had a plan. It is selfish to leave your children without any direction on how to handle their affairs. It's also irresponsible to leave it for someone else to handle for your family. It is an absolute burden to leave plans unfinished for someone else to manage.

In this section, I'm describing what is included in an estate plan. Once you have an estate plan, I'd say you are as close to an adult as you could probably get because it takes great responsibility to make those decisions and execute those documents. These documents are hard to prepare, and many push them off because they don't want to ever think about it. In the documents are a trust, an identified power of attorney, a healthcare proxy, and a will.

A **trust** is a family asset vehicle that holds your family's assets, like a house or investment management accounts. A **power of attorney** handles your monetary affairs if you become incapacitated and helps file your tax return while you are still living but unable to make those decisions for yourself. A **healthcare proxy** is someone who makes medical decisions for you if you are unable to make them for yourself. This document is rather important, and I see all my well-established clients get this document done for their children once they are eighteen years old. At eighteen, you are technically an adult, and if you were to get hurt, a doctor would not be able to talk to your parent figures because you are considered an adult. This is rather important for students that are going away for school. The last standard form is a **will,** which outlines your wishes for how the assets you've worked hard to build will be passed on—to support both your future and the generations that follow.

It is an incredible thing to be so selfless and set the next generation of your family up for success by leaving them a nest egg to have a leg up in the world. The will, as part of the estate plan, includes guardianship provisions. If something were to happen to one or both of your parent figures, this specifies your parent figures' wishes on who would take care of you and your siblings. It's typically a close relative or friend of your parent figures.

A lot of estate planning is very complex and detailed and requires a lot more explanation than what we're able to get into in this book. It's okay if the material seems overwhelming; when the time comes, there are many professionals who can help you get through it. Some stuff in this book is "common sense," like hygiene, and some of it might go over your head right now. Just know it would be really smart to have these financial and family conversations with your partner or yourself at some point in time that feels right without pushing it off too far. An estate plan is like life insurance—you need it when you don't have it in place. So be proactive. Do not let yourself get in the way of being organized and successful.

Taking Responsibility, One Step at a Time

Becoming an adult comes with a ton of new responsibilities. It is imperative to remember to take them one step at a time. Instead of worrying about this immense pressure of these mounting responsibilities that are typically gradually learned over a couple of years, learn to take them one step at a time with the help of your family. Your family—whether chosen or traditional—is probably the best group of people you can have these conversations with.

When realizing all of this, sometimes there's an immense pressure that you put on yourself. Sometimes you think about how much it costs to maintain the lifestyle you were accustomed to by your family. Or you dream of the lifestyle you want and think about the mountain you will have to climb to get there. When you think about your childhood, it might feel extremely intimidating to provide the lifestyle you want or to mirror your parent figures with your own children. Sometimes you feel like, *WOW, the only way I will be able to afford myself is if I do the same profession that my parent figures do.* I wonder if that's why a lot of kids like us follow their parent figures' footsteps with career choices in the first place? That would be an interesting survey—tying quality of life pressures back to career choices based on childhood.

Someday you will start to think about all of the fixed costs that your parent figures had just to raise you, and maybe your parent figures didn't just have you, but they had other children as well that were in other activities, too. It can be intimidating to think about how successful your parent figures were or were not in providing you with a childhood, but there are a couple of things you need to remind yourself of.

The first thing you realize is that your parent figures, by the time they reach their forties or fifties, are already well into their careers—often having climbed the ladder in their industry or company. They were students for twenty or so years and in a career for twenty or so years. They've climbed this corporate ladder enough that they have seniority in their jobs to have the flexibility to pick you up from practice or coach your sports team/drama club or drop you off at school and make sure you get on the bus.

You have to remember that your parent figures are older and that they've worked really hard. Consistency is a huge quality that you should look for in someone when you are finding your partner. I'd bet that kids who had a great childhood often had parent figures who were consistent—emotionally, financially, spiritually, and in other important ways.

The second thing you should remember is you need to be gentle with yourself and not be so hard on yourself. This is easier said than done. Some of the lessons in this book are things you might hear from your parent figures or read elsewhere—but many of them, you'll have to learn for yourself, in your own time and in your own way.

It's okay to learn things on your own time in your own life, but the purpose of all of the self-help books, parent figures, role models, or mentors in your industry is to learn from their mistakes. Take what they've already learned and absorb their stories and lessons; if you really take in the lessons from others, it will only propel you forward with fewer mistakes that you will have to make on your own. I hope you really think about that. I hope you listen to people's stories, advice, and goals. It will only **slingshot** you farther and faster.

The third thing that you need to remind yourself when it comes to the intimidation of how your parent figures have done so much for you is to be grateful for it and to pay it forward. You will probably never be able to repay your parent figures for everything they've done. Unless you take care of them when they are sick and older, you could become very wealthy someday and buy your mom that beach house she always wanted. (I am hoping I can buy my mom the beach house she wants and has been talking about for years with this book.) But the biggest thing your parent figures want for you is to be happy, to marry well, to have a great life, to have purpose in society, and to pay parenting forward with your children (not to mention, make them grandparents someday).

Take some time to think about who you are within your own family and what you bring and contribute to your inner society or bubble. Also, think about who your parent figures are in relation to society and what their added value is or who they help day in and day out.

I know what you are thinking. *My knowing my family's ins and outs is common sense. I've lived with them. I know them.* Yes, you do. But have you thought about who they are not only to you but also to society? Your family was your first introduction to society, and society will gradually introduce you to more and more as you get older. Your network in society starts with how you foster the building blocks of your core network.

Your family is your first core society beyond yourself. Your friends are your second.

KEY TAKEAWAYS:

- **Your First Society.** Your family—no matter how imperfect—is your first experience of community. They shape how you see the world and how you show up in it. While family dynamics can be complicated, being there for your core people matters. They were your first society, and that foundation stays with you.
- **Estate Planning.** Legal documents like prenuptial agreements and estate plans aren't just for the wealthy—they're essential tools for protecting your future. Think of them like insurance: If you wait until you need them, it's already too late. Planning ahead is a responsibility, not just for yourself but for those who may one day have to navigate your affairs.
- **Taking Responsibility, Gradually.** Becoming an adult is a process, not a switch. It's easy to feel pressure when you compare yourself to your parent figures or the life they gave you—but they had decades to get there. Focus on learning step by step, asking questions, and being kind to yourself along the way. Responsibility isn't about perfection—it's about progress and showing up.

CHAPTER 7

FRIENDS: BUILDING YOUR CIRCLE (IT'S BIGGER THAN YOU THINK)

Your second introduction into society was friends. Whether you realize it or not, you had started to develop friends at a young age, most likely with your siblings, cousins, friends you met in preschool, or your parent figures' friends who had kids around the same age as you. We all have those family friends who we call aunt or uncle, but you never really understood why because they weren't blood related.

You can never have too many friends.

So, if you are off to an advanced education for a few years, you will probably tell your parent figures you were at the library studying when you were out partying with your friends. Don't worry—most of us have done it. Your parent figures know already. Believe it or not, you were doing something super important. You were actually networking, and that was good for your personal brand, too. No harm, no foul. You're young. Be young. But also, be nice to everyone. It's so underrated and doesn't take much.

Friendships & Personal Growth

It becomes important to keep your network strong and stay in touch with people throughout the years. It also feels better to pay a friend for their services than a stranger because you know your money is going to support their family. There's something to be said for putting your community/town first and working with these local professionals in the future. That's why before the G word (graduation), everyone starts to act nice—so you remember them as being nice. Just be nice the whole time. No one ever wants to feel left out. We all have our place in society and within a friend group.

ON-THE-JOB TIP: Be nice to everyone.

You will be making new friends the rest of your life; you will have your preschool friends, you will have your grammar school friends, you will have your Girl Scout friends, you will have your high school and college friends, work friends, your kid's friend's parents as friends, and so on.

All of these different friend groups will be your network to rely on outside of your family. Your network of friends will go into various types of career fields, so the more friends you have, the more exposure you have to different fields. Your network is friends that turn into professionals in different industries. So be friendly with everyone regardless of if they go into a trade, advanced education, or right to work. Everyone needs a hair stylist, an electrician, and a plumber for those houses that you are all going to start saving for while you live below your means in your childhood bedroom. You'll also need that friend who can do your tax return and clean your teeth.

Your network of all your friends will, one day, around your forties, all be (hopefully) wildly successful in their respective careers. That's pretty cool to think about. "Wildly successful" can be interpreted in many ways, including owning your own business, being an employee and being able to shut your computer on Fridays at five p.m., being an executive, and so on. Everyone will have their own story on how they found their success through career progression and what they attribute their success to. Especially because you still think of regular old Connor as the beer funnel king from college—but now he's out here running a law firm.

> **ON-THE-JOB TIP:** There is a two-drink max at a work event. Or better yet, just save the fun for later and be present at the work event with a water.

Friends are very valuable, and they teach you a lot about yourself. They will tell you who you are. Especially if you are having a hard time figuring out who you are yourself from earlier. Honestly, they will tell you when you've messed up or you are wrong for doing something. Friends will keep you honest when family may not, because friends have nothing to lose if they lose a friendship over it, whereas your family might dance around topics like that because they still have to see you at holidays.

Do you remember hearing "You are who your friends are," growing up? Who are your friends right now? What are they doing in life, and what are you doing in life? Are you who your friends are? What is everyone's earning potential? The movies from Hollywood aren't too far off. They may over-stereotype the lunch tables in about every high school movie, but everyone is with their people.

These fundamental relationships in society have helped shape you and also stereotyped you a little bit. Yes, stereotyping can be bad, but it's also good. Sometimes it helps. You actually understand more of who you are by stereotyping. You need to take these common hobbies and interests and keep finding friends these ways as you mature (hopefully) in life. The students that are mature have gotten this far in the book. Congrats. We can take a moment to giggle at the students who didn't get past page eighteen. Good luck to them.

You made connections the whole way through with people who find joy in the same thing you do. Keep finding joy. Don't make time as you get older for things that don't give you joy. You will overall just be a better person in society if you are true to you and your friends.

Being a Good Friend

Something that might be hard is remembering how to be a good friend, and I am here to remind you that it's not as hard as it might seem. Friendships can ebb and flow, and expectations of different relationships can sometimes be the straw that breaks the camel's back. At the end of the day, you need to remember that you want to have as many friends as possible. You can NEVER have too many friends.

Sometimes making friends comes easy to people, and sometimes it's not, but **what makes having a good group of friends easy is being true to yourself.** Don't be the person who is a try-hard to fit in with the "right" group of people. You don't need to try to fit in with true friends.

When I started my first job, I went to my first real-world networking event. Yes, it's lamer than it sounds while also being extremely intimidating. My mentor at work said you want to be able to walk into a room and know most of the people.

The only way that is going to happen in your respective industry is to start talking to people and finding common ground with them. You obviously won't find this with everyone or become BFFs off the bat, BUT there is nothing wrong with an acquaintance.

Networking events can be challenging; it always feels as though the real people that you need to meet aren't at the networking events because they are working or spending time with family. You don't need to exclusively network at a bar only. For instance, I had met someone through mutual clients. After our first meeting with this client, they made a point every year to take me out to lunch. I thought it was so . . . strange at first. Why would they want to go to lunch with me? I'm not the client. I'm the boring accountant. So, I blatantly asked, and their response was sharp. They said that they were in the service industry, so if they showed me how they treat me by staying in touch basically once a quarter, I would refer them more business because I would know that's how they would treat the client. WITH LOTS OF ATTENTION. As if they were family and friends, because isn't that what you do with friends? Go to lunch and talk on the phone? It seems so simple . . . but that's how they earned more money—by being consistent. Now, I try to embody that as well with my email calendar reminders.

How do you get to know people to the best of your ability in these different situations? Are you an introvert or an extrovert? Do you like getting to know people over lunch, or are you better at cocktail hours in a big group at the end of the day?

It is not hard to smile or to greet people with a smile. Think about how comforting it is when someone smiles at you and says hello. Isn't that the number one rule when it comes to sales? *Smile!* Be that person; be the person who always shows up for other people's successes. Because you want people to show up

ON THE-JOB TIP: Sit up straight and smile with confidence! I bet you just corrected your posture.

for you when you've made a big move in life.

Overall, just have compassion and empathy for people. Sometimes you don't learn that right away or the gravity of what that means because you are in your twenties and heavily focused on yourselves right now. You are learning how to be responsible for just you. At the end of the day, we should all have respect for people. We should all respect people and humans because we all go through human experiences in life. So when you look at someone in their eyes, meet them with compassion and understanding.

Being a good friend means showing up for friends during the hard times in life. Reaching out and connecting with a friend when a pet or family member passes, when they lose their job, or when they are struggling with some sort of change shows you care. This is what adults do for each other—they demonstrate friendships that are reciprocal.

It's that simple saying that we all already know: "Treat others how you would want to be treated." Even if someone is not nice to you, it says more about how you handle the situation and meet them with kindness rather than trying to hurt them the way they hurt you.

A good friend shows up for other friends at happy events, too, like when they get married, when they have a baby shower, or when they buy a new car. Those are the true friends who are showing up to congratulate you on your successes, and those friends aren't comparing either. Friends might not be there for the day-to-day struggles, but a good friend should be there for the happy things that matter to you. Remember everyone has something different that really matters to them that they would expect you to show up at. Knowing your friends well enough to know what's important to them is part of being a good friend.

Having good friends is important, especially when they are around your age. It helps when everyone in your group is going through similar stages of life together. It's also great to be friends with older people to get wisdom from them, but it may be a little hard to relate to them.

Take the time to make a pro and con list of your different friends' qualities. Think about which traits you admire and would like to develop in yourself because you find them likable or valuable. From everyone you meet in life, take note of both their good and bad traits. Learn from who they are and how they act in society, then use those lessons to improve yourself—for the greater good.

Someone once taught me this. They told me that they first did this with both of their parent figures, and they would think about the good qualities of their mom and dad, and they would just take those from them, and all the bad stuff they would just leave behind.

Then they would start to do this with their childhood friends, and they realized that their childhood friends weren't going anywhere, but they really wanted to keep developing, so they made new friends when they moved on and went to college and their coworkers, and so on.

What I'm saying is always evaluate your friends and your relation to them. It's always good to do a little check-in with them and yourself so you can be the best helpful friend possible to those in society that mean the most to you.

Continuously spread love and joy to everyone that you meet. Radiating positivity will only attract well-rounded and positive friends. Fostering the good starts within yourself.

KEY TAKEAWAYS

- **Friends: Your Chosen Circle in Society.** Friends become your chosen family and an essential part of your social network. You'll form different levels of friendships throughout life—embrace as many as possible and nurture these connections. Strive to be a reliable resource and a "walking phone book" who brings people together.

- **Friendships and Personal Growth.** As you grow and evolve, so will your friendships. Regularly reflect on who your friends are and who you are becoming. Surround yourself with those whose values and qualities inspire you to grow into your best self.
- **Show Up and Cultivate Mutual Respect.** Being a good friend means showing up—not just in the good times, but especially in the hard ones. Adulthood calls for honoring relationships with mutual respect, support, and consistency. Healthy friendships are built on giving and receiving care, and as you mature, these bonds become a foundation for resilience and shared success.

CHAPTER 8

PARTNERS: LOVE, LOGIC & A LITTLE BIT OF MATH

The right partner is someone you cherish spending time with, and it always feels like there's never enough time with them. Two imperfect people, united in life and on the same team. Your role is to understand them as deeply as they take responsibility to understand you.

I think everyone has a moment in their life that makes them realize what they want in a partner that stands out to them. Good listener, quality caregiver, loving, kind, affectionate, family-oriented, professional, respectful, empathetic, funny, good communicator, dependable, supportive, independent, mature, and accepting are incredible shared qualities that we all look for in a partner. One quality might be more important to you than the other, but they all hold equal value when you are looking for someone who is the full picture. None of us is perfect, and having the universe put someone in front of you who is accepting of that fact creates a great foundation to build a life off of.

Finding the Right Partner

Society wants you to find a partner to grow old with who is around your age because you will be going through similar life stages at the same time. It should be said that society also pushes partnerships because they'd like to sustain population growth. Obviously not everyone needs a partner to be happy. And not everyone needs to have kids to be happy. This is a good time to value what a good partner is and to understand what will work for you in your future. Picking the right person to partner with is a huge responsibility.

I think there is a sense of ease that parent figures have once one of their children finds the right partner, because then the parent feels as though they aren't leaving this earth without their child being loved by someone. That love might not ever equate to how much the parent figures love their child, but if you pick the right partner, it's pretty darn close.

As easy as this topic may seem, it's pretty complex because we are all so different. It's easy to say it's not hard to find a nice, smart, driven, enthusiastic, upbeat, good-looking, athletic, and gainfully employed partner. But it's different for everyone. You will attract what you put out into the world. You may even attract someone who admires a quality that you have. Just remember that you are put on this earth to live your life to the absolute fullest—and if you so choose, you are also able to share a life with someone.

This person whom you choose to be your partner is your whole world and part of your society. While some are worried about carat, cut, clarity, and color, the majority of us are looking for communication, commitment, comedy, and character. Know the difference between the four Cs! It's not all about keeping up and flaunting your life for people you don't talk to daily.

ON-THE-JOB TIP: Be professional. You aren't at work to find a partner.

It seems like most breakups happen close to the one-year mark in the relationship. It is one of those marks in time that is very telling because you have spent four seasons with them and really gotten to know them and what they want in life. Always keep this internal deadline in your mind and evaluate the situation. You won't need to level up in the relationship to prove anything after one year, but you should have a conversation with yourself to see if it's worth continuing.

Common things we all want in a respectful partner are arguing respectfully with regard to their delivery and approaching the situation in a calm voice; being a problem solver and not pointing the finger at anyone; having similar goals and respect for individual goals; displaying honesty and continuously earning trust; showing poise in high-stress situations like needing to go to the hospital or decision-making environments (because when I am older, my mom won't be at the hospital with me—it'll be my partner); genuinely liking how they make you feel when you're with them; laughing; and, most importantly, having fun every day and making the most of every day together.

In a partnership, the understanding of having great success is knowing there's a balancing act between the percentage of effort that is put in. In theory this percentage over your lifetime will equal fifty-fifty. There will be some days where you contribute 10 percent and your partner does 90 percent, then vice versa. We all have our bad days, so when those days come around, your partner might make dinner and clean the kitchen and empty the dishwasher if you are feeling ill. Then the next month your partner might be working toward a promotion, and they are working late nights, so you are managing more within your relationship since they are less available. This kind of percentage split is normal and totally fine—but being able to recognize the difference between that and a situation where you're being taken advantage of or where the effort just isn't mutual is key. That awareness is often the clearest sign of where things are headed: Splitsville.

The majority of this is all figured out through trial and error with dating different people at different stages of life. Following is a list of questions to ask yourself when it comes to what you want in a partnership:

1. Are they goal-oriented?
2. Do they want a career of their own?
3. Are they reliable? Do they pick up the phone when you call?
4. Do they want a family?
5. Did they learn your love languages?
6. Do they tell you they love you?
7. Do they encourage you in your goals?
8. Do they love you for who you are and not try and change you?
9. Do you care enough about them to learn their love languages?
10. How do they picture retirement? Are they good savers for retirement?
11. How do they celebrate holidays?
12. Do they make your life easier, even in small ways?
13. How do they picture celebrating holidays once married or with children?
14. Do they think ahead and help you with things?
15. Do they help lighten your mental load?
16. Do they mind hanging out with your family?
17. Do they want to invest in you to build a life with you?
18. Do they know how to handle you when you are having a temper tantrum and still love you anyways?
19. Do you like their friends?

20. Can you sit in silence with them and still feel completely content—not bored?
21. Do they remember the little things that make you happy?
22. When you're doing something fun without them, do you find yourself wishing they were there too—even though you're still having a good time?
23. Are they kind to others, not just to you?
24. Do you trust them to be your healthcare proxy and make medical decisions for you?
25. Do they have your back when you are not in the room?
26. Do they love you? Unconditionally?
27. Do they put their phone down when they are talking with you? Are they all ears?
28. Are they an equal partner that complements you and your life?
29. Do they save before they spend?
30. Do you feel safe with them?
31. Can you be honest with them?
32. Can you voice concerns, thoughts, or ideas to them with confidence?
33. Are they your biggest cheerleader? Are they on your team? Do they support your ambitions?

You want someone who has the same morals and good qualities and characteristics that complement your own. Getting to know their family and friends gives you valuable insight into their world—the society they come from, how they were raised, and who shaped them. It really gives you a clear picture on who they are.

There are a lot of nerves and angst when meeting your partner's family for the first time. Everybody is trying to be on their best behavior. So obviously, you cannot judge a book by its cover, and you have to get to know them as the relationship grows.

Take the time to analyze their characteristics, how they operate under pressure, or even see how they gather for the holidays. When you are a student, your parent figures really make the magic of the holidays what it is. They work tirelessly to make the days special. They get a few days off to then cook and clean and spend time with their crazy family. Make sure you find the right partner who is able to balance this all and still make the magic of bringing people together, especially for the big holidays.

Whether it's creating a fair holiday schedule to split time between families or bringing both families together for a celebration, putting in that effort matters—it makes those special occasions smoother and more enjoyable for everyone.

At the end of the day, you want someone who complements you and your goals. This is the "stuff" that isn't talked about with your parent figures at the dinner table or at school with the teacher. Let's be honest, if your parent figures tried to tell you to pick a good partner or expressed they didn't love your current partner so much, you would be insulted and rebel. I'm here to tell you to consider this list of questions and analyze your situation and what you want. Some people don't have role-model relationships to look up to, but **we all intuitively know what we want out of a partner. So listen to your inner self.**

Partnership & Finances

It is important to talk about money with your partner and make sure you are on the same budget and understanding to live below your means in order to grow a nest egg for retirement, unless you want to work forever. Financial freedom is accomplished slowly over time. It is acquired only in an instant if you win Powerball. It can disappear just as quickly if you don't manage it wisely—especially if you spend the principal instead of living off the income it generates for you and future generations.

No money, no honey. If someone doesn't have a job, the odds are that they don't have a honey. It is super important to make sure that this person—the one you're legally bound to and committing to spend the rest of your life with—is financially savvy or at least willing to learn how to be savvier.

You don't want to marry someone who lives beyond their means and doesn't save well. When you earn more, it doesn't mean you should spend more. If your family is warning you not to marry someone or saying they're not a good fit, it's worth considering. Your parent figures have likely been through similar experiences, and, whether you want to admit it or not, they often know you better than you know yourself—especially at this stage in life. Most of us are guilty of forgetting that.

Wealth, status, and ego have been hot topics for centuries. It is funny to joke about marrying wealthy people because life would be so much easier if you just had money. Sarcasm. And this statement is, in fact, *false*.

If you marry for money, you will pay the rest of your life.

You could totally marry someone who is very wealthy. You could work your whole life, save every penny, and still not be as wealthy as you could be if you had just married someone with money. But just know there have been many people before you who have thought they could buy their happiness, and it doesn't work.

Learn from people before you and pick your partner by having your gut speak to you. Yes, you should also pick your partner with your heart and mind, but you need to think of your gut as your other brain.

Your Partnerships and Personal Balance Sheets

They say every couple argues about three things: sex, children, and money. Gratification and wealth are made over the long haul with combined morals and practices. As we discussed earlier, one thing that wealthy clients do is they document their *personal balance sheet*. These become even more important when you enter a partnership. Earlier we talked about understanding these sheets as a young person and a young professional just starting out. Look back at the example and the sheet you mocked up at that time.

Now let's consider what your balance sheet may look like at the next stage in life, let's say in another five to ten years. You are established or just starting out in your career/graduated. Your personal balance sheet might look something like this:

Personal Balance Sheet for YOU in the Future
Assets: Salary ~$55,000 Car ~$10,000 (Remember, cars depreciate in value.) 401(k) ~$5,000 Savings Account ~$3,000 Checking Account ~$500 Residential Property ~$350,000 ROTH IRA ~$500 Emergency Fund ~$2,000
Liabilities: Car Loan ~$9,000 (This is less because you'd presumably pay it down.) Mortgage ~$345,000 Student Loans ~$70,000 (This is less because you'd presumably pay it down.) Credit Card Debt ~$100 Partner

What do you want your future balance sheet to look like? What do you want your future partner's balance sheet to look like?

Yes, your right partner is a liability (I hope you laughed) because it costs money to keep them around even if they have their own job. When I say "liability," I mean it costs money to do activities with them, and they can be financially draining. It's expensive to do activities with someone on the weekends. Even if your partner does have a career and a well-paying job to cover their cost of living, they might not contribute to a 401(k) or save for the future with or without you, which can pose a problem if you are both not on the same page financially. Making sure your partner has strong financial literacy is important to your future.

At some point, you are going to want your partner to fill out a personal balance sheet. I'm not saying on the second date to pull out a napkin and make your partner walk through their personal balance sheet at a restaurant, but at some point the conversation will be right and you'll want to have this personal balance sheet conversation. Maybe a good time to have a more in-depth conversation about money would be at least around the one year mark, a pivotal milestone in most relationships, as I mentioned before. You have had a year to observe their spending habits that hopefully mirror yours. By then, you will have a good sense on what their spending and saving habits are even without doing a personal balance sheet. At that point, after four seasons with them, it will be clear to you if you want them around and if they add value to your life.

When you're ready, you should both fill your sheets out independently. Then you will put them side-by-side. Assuming your relationship may progress further, these materials would actually also come in handy as the first exhibit of a prenuptial agreement called an "asset disclosure list." I've provided an example of a mock couple's balance sheets.

Personal Balance Sheet for YOU	Personal Balance Sheet for Your Partner
Assets:	Assets:
Liabilities:	Liabilities:

Personal Balance Sheet for YOU	Personal Balance Sheet for Your Partner
<u>Assets:</u> Salary ~$85,000 (Your salary has increased.) Car ~$8,000 (Remember, cars depreciate in value.) 401(k) ~$10,000 (You matched your 401(k) when you first started and every year increase it 2 percent.) Savings Account ~$4,000 Checking Account ~$500 Residential Property ~$375,000 (In this scenario, you did some projects, so your house appreciated.) ROTH IRA ~$500 Emergency Fund ~$2,000	<u>Assets:</u> Salary ~$60,000 401(k) ~$34,000 (Your partner is currently maxing out their 401(k) after a few years of working.) Checking Account ~$2,000 Car ~$25,000 (Remember, cars depreciate in value.)
<u>Liabilities:</u> Car Loan ~$6,000 (This is less because you'd presumably pay it down.) Mortgage ~$335,000 (You have paid down some of your mortgage.) Student Loans ~$62,000 (This is less because you'd presumably pay it down.) Credit Card Debt ~$300	<u>Liabilities:</u> Car Loan ~$0 Student Loans ~$120,000 (In this scenario, your partner is aggressively paying down their debt since they are living with parent figures. They are "paying rent" through planned budgeting and putting it toward their loan debt.) Credit Card Debt ~$0

As you can see in the example, the goal is to see your assets increasing and your liabilities decreasing. Your salary has gone up with you also prioritizing paying down your liabilities. What do you think of the example? If this partner has all the qualities that you admire, do they financially look like a good fit for you? Does it seem they have good financial morals and goals?

Yes, getting married is glamorous. But it's like prom. There is a lot of buildup, and at the end it is just a party and paperwork. The paperwork being the marriage license and, if you so wish, a prenuptial and postnuptial agreements. Remember, when you marry someone, you also take on all their debt, too. If you do a personal balance sheet with someone and they have a $60,000 salary and a 401(k), they own their car, and maybe they have an apartment or a house so they have good credit, then on the liability section they probably have a car loan, but that's normal. That's "good" debt, but if they have several thousands of dollars in student loan debt, maybe you have conversations with them about what their plans are to pay it down responsibly. Are they going to pay them down before you get married or before you have children? Are they expecting you to pay their debts? Would you live off of one income and pay down debt with one of your other incomes until you plan to have children?

There's a lot of pride in paying off your debts. So I'm not saying dump the person if they have student loan debt, but what I'm saying is if they plan to have the student loan debt the rest of their life, it might be an issue because you're eventually going to have kids and a house (if you both want that), and all of this debt will accumulate and will just completely drown you and hold you back from doing other things in life. A bank won't give you a loan for a house with a lot of other debts. Remember, a bank is looking for your bankability. Meaning they are looking for you to have that liquidity in order to grant you a loan. That's why budgeting is so helpful with planning for our next step. You are saving liquid assets to be bankable.

I can't count how many clients we recommend a prenuptial agreement to—only for them to skip it, then email us at tax time asking if they can file "Married Filing Separately" because they're worried about being tied to their partner's debts. News flash, you are too late! You should have listened to the advice given or asked more questions to understand it fully. What's yours is theirs, and what's theirs is yours. Don't wait to have these important conversations with your partner until after you have signed the paperwork.

There used to be a stigma around the word "prenup." I think a lot of people only thought it was for the wealthy, but it's not. Your partner may be in law school or medical school, and you decided to invest in their penny stocks now with the hopes of their careers taking off well beyond their student loan debts that were on their first personal balance sheet. A prenup isn't always about protecting your income—it can also be about safeguarding an inheritance, ensuring it stays within your family or bloodline.

I think society in general has gotten smarter. I know I laughed when I wrote that sentence, but they have. Couples realize that there are already established rules regarding marriage and estates, as well as differences among state laws. If you decide to not get a prenup (or estate plan), you will have to follow the already established state governing rules. Most people don't want to follow those rules and want to create their own morals or rules in writing. That's all you are actually doing—changing what is already established to fit your situation. Not everyone's situation is cookie-cutter; hence, personalized planning is needed.

For instance, in Massachusetts the law right now is if you are married for more than ten years, it doesn't matter who made the money or who worked; if after ten years your marriage leads to a divorce, everything is split fifty-fifty. If you have a prenup—and possibly even a postnup—you and your partner can agree to terms that override state law, so you're not strictly bound by it.

On the flip side, showing your assets and liabilities is also what it looks like when you get divorced. You have to show and break out all of your cost of living expenses and income when you're getting divorced and going through family court in order to prove you need to receive or give spousal support.

The well-established also use a personal balance sheet to compare a business's balance sheet to an individual's personal balance sheet. This example is for someone who is an entrepreneur and owns their own business. For example, if you went to dental school or went into a trade, there is no class on how to run your own business or practice business ethics. There is no class on how to read a balance sheet and income statement. You have to go and pay top dollar for a really good accountant who provides added value for YOU and your small business. Most of the time accountants are billing hourly and only focused on the prior year and not helping with tax planning for the future. This is because they are always doing the return and looking at the financials for the previous year. Here is a simple way to evaluate your business monthly and yearly without having to do a math formula to evaluate the health of your business.

You, as the business owner, have two balance sheets to deal with: your business's and your personal one. The next two charts illustrate your two tax returns you file in a simpler manner.

Personal Balance Sheet for YOU	Personal Balance Sheet for Your Business
Assets:	Assets:
Liabilities:	Liabilities:

Personal Balance Sheet for YOU	Personal Balance Sheet for Your Business
Assets: Salary ~$100,000–$300,000 (A business owner pays their own salary first even though they own the company.) House ~$550,000 Investment Account ~$200,000 529 Plans ~$30,000 Savings Account ~$20,000 401(k) ~$400,000 Car ~$40,000	Assets: Cash ~$75,000 (This is the total after paying all the bills at the end of the month.) Company Car ~$75,000 Equipment ~$60,000 Employees Office Building ~$650,000
Liabilities: Mortgage ~$300,000 Credit Card ~$4,000 Children	Liabilities: Credit Card ~$2,000 Building Mortgage ~$400,000 Employees' Payroll ~$200,000 Business Loans

As an example, let's stick with you owning your own business—let's say it's a dental office. The previous balance sheets are examples of what it would look like. Remember, we are illustrating an example for someone in their thirties or forties who is more established and has worked hard to acquire their license, practice, and wealth. How do the numbers look? Is the owner living beyond their means with too many liabilities on both sides that are larger numbers than the money coming in? If they were married, we would have their partner on here as well if they worked.

Seeing these two balance sheets side-by-side is imperative. It is more common to not see more assets piled up on the business side. The biggest mistake I see small business owners make is keeping too much cash (an asset) in their business. The business owner doesn't move the cash from the business's asset column on the balance sheet to the asset column in their personal balance sheet. They simply aren't growing their personal assets. This is because they are like an ostrich with their head in the sand and elbows deep in their business, worrying about having it operate a certain way to have that cash in the business in the first place. Remember, when you own your own business, you are accountable to more people than just one boss. They are accountable to too many people day in and day out, and the last thing they are worrying about is their retirement because they are taking their health and stamina for granted.

It is like having all your cash invested in one concentrated stock account. It doesn't get you anywhere because you are not diversified and managing your risk in that one asset. It is also a huge liability to keep that much cash in the business because if the business is sued for something, the person seeking damages has access to a lot of the assets or cash that you leave in the business.

I know the business owner isn't managing their money or cash flow well professionally if that is the case, which means they don't know how to do it personally, either. I know their money isn't working for them in multiple avenues to increase their quality of life LIKE THE WEALTHY DO. In this example, the dentist is not concentrated in their investments. Their first investment is the business. They are pulling the cash out and paying themselves and investing that cash in other avenues like an investment account, rental properties, other businesses, etc. It's like Monopoly—they are buying assets that provide them more assets. Get as many hotels as you can by having your money work for you and providing you more money!

So we tax plan for the future and rip that cash out and invest it in different ways. I know you are dying to know how the wealthy save or diversify that money, so here are some examples after retirement accounts have been fully maxed out: 529 plans for children or grandchildren, annual gift exclusion for beneficiaries, rental properties, funding investment accounts, investing in other businesses, trusts, and so on.

It isn't complex. It isn't easy (otherwise everyone would manage their money this way). It isn't extravagant, either. There aren't some crazy, fancy estate or tax laws that these people are using that you can't use.

So this personal balance sheet is huge, and you should do it annually when you file your tax return. Year over year, you're going to be able to compare and show how much you have grown financially as an individual and also as a family with your partner and with your business.

You could even do a mock personal balance sheet to illustrate for yourself what you want your life to be like when you set goals/

retirement. This works like creating a mock résumé to show the experience you need for the career you want. You can also use it as a vision board reminder. A lot of wealthy people do this with a mock résumé and mock personal balance sheet. Here is an example of a retirement goal personal balance sheet for your future:

Personal Balance Sheet for YOUR Retirement
Assets: New House Boat Sports Car 401(k) IRAs Rental Property Income Business Ownership Social Security Investment Accounts 529 Plans/UTMAs Trust Accounts Petty Cash
Liabilities: Boat Loan Car Loan Mortgage Credit Card Auto Loans

How do you want your retirement to look? Does your vision match your partner's?

This little tool is super helpful and imperative to teach to your own kids, too. Society is dependent on how you grew up, and having strong financial conversations around money is really important. A good relationship isn't all about money, is it? No, but it might be one of the biggest reasons people get divorced.

So even if your parent figures didn't have strong conversations with you about money, you need to take it upon yourself to make sure that you pick the right partner who has all great qualities and knows how to manage money, or better yet, hire a professional in society to help.

KEY TAKEAWAYS

- **Choose the Right Partner for You.** The "right" partner isn't about perfection—it's about what's right for you. Pay attention to how you feel around them, how they handle life's challenges, and whether your values align. The strength of your relationship depends on this foundation.
- **Align on Goals and Finances Early.** Share financial goals and have open conversations about money. Create a strong starting point for a lasting partnership. Whether it's saving, spending, or planning for the future, being on the same page helps prevent tension and builds mutual trust.
- **Build Personal Balance Sheets Together.** Creating personal balance sheets as a couple gives you a clear view of where you both stand financially. It's not just about numbers—it's about making sure you're on the same financial trajectory and working toward shared goals with transparency and intention.

CHAPTER 9

YOUR ROLE IN SOCIETY: HOW WE SHOW UP, PAY UP & SHAPE WHAT'S NEXT

Many can argue that society is run by a lot of different things. I've heard it all, from social media to aliens. Each citizen in each country has incredible pride for where they were born and raised. If you are from the United States and you think back to your US history class, you would have hopefully learned that each citizen in the United States of America has a civic duty to the greater good that is governed by the US government. Beyond that, each citizen within each country has a civic duty to themselves, their neighborhood, their family, their religion, their state, and their country.

We as individuals can obviously govern ourselves, our parent figures can govern us while we are living under their roof, and our significant others can also have some governance over our well-being. We can govern our businesses, but it's equally important to understand how we're governed as citizens. Two often-overlooked civic responsibilities are understanding how our government functions and how taxation works—both of which are essential for contributing to the greater good.

Politics & Voting

Whether we would like to admit it or not, the government of your country is a huge factor in how society is run. In the United States, there are three branches of government: judicial, legislative, and executive. From a thirty-thousand-foot view, the executive branch is the president, the judicial branch is the US Supreme Court, and the legislative branch holds the House of Representatives and the Senate.

The number of state representatives in the house is dependent upon the state's per capita, and they are elected every two years. There are two senators from each state, and they are elected every six years. A lot of power is held within these three branches, and not just in America—these representatives have an impact on other countries as well.

The two parties that make up these branches are the Democratic and Republican parties. Throughout history, these two parties have had a lot of contention. We can learn from history. We can be even better than history. We need these two parties for the greater good with checks and balances. Not one person or party is perfect. We need each other. We don't have to like everything the other party says, but we need to get things done together and negotiate for the greater good.

As an adult, you should expect many divisive conversations to come up regarding this topic. You are an adult and need to handle them responsibly. At the Thanksgiving table and business conference table, don't bring up politics, and don't overshare your opinions while you're still in the process of forming them. You want to be neutral and professional in all situations. Leave it at the door. In my line of work, this conversation comes up a lot. A lot, a lot. That's because many new bills that are passed change the tax code on how individuals and businesses are taxed. Do you think I only have clients aligned to one political party? No. We all have the liberty to run our own businesses the way we want. Remember, we want to have as many friends as possible. If you own your own business, don't you want to have as many customers as possible, regardless of their beliefs? Sure, you are providing a service or good to a particular audience, but can't it be inclusive to everyone? Everyone's money is green after all . . .

What can you do now since you are taking initiative of your life as an adult? Start with registering to vote and register with a political party that represents the values that are most important to you. Don't know what that looks like yet? That's okay. Register as an independent or unaffiliated voter. Maybe your opinion changes depending on who is running for a position at a certain time. You can also stay an independent permanently.

We need to be good role models even if we don't see role models ourselves within society. Do you remember when the coaches at your middle school baseball or soccer games would argue with each other or the referees if there was a bad call? I sure do; it would get very awkward, very fast. It didn't serve anyone. Everyone just left. Pathetic. The likelihood that someone on your T-ball team was going pro was very slim. We were all just kids there to have fun. The kids typically wouldn't get involved in the fight because we all knew enough not to, and we needed to be role models for ourselves. Be like the kids and know better than to get involved in a fight over politics that no one is going to "win." Being an adult means knowing when to choose your battles. We all have our own opinions and morals that are important to us, and that's what's so beautiful about our society; we can all learn from each other's perspectives without a WWE SmackDown. If someone professionally or personally won't let up on the conversation because they want to try and prove they are smart and follow politics or start a fight with you, then just say, "I don't want to discuss this topic with you. My mom taught me to never talk about sex, money, or politics at the dinner table." It works every time. Don't be the screaming coach on the sidelines; be the kids in right field pulling the grass out of the ground when it comes to this topic in the professional world.

The idea that we should all be ethical, hold high integrity for ourselves, and be independent thinkers should be the framework for how you vote for someone. Voting is a blessing and our civic duty. To think that only two generations before us, our grandmothers did not have the right to vote is absolutely wild. I vow to vote in any and every election because it is my civic duty to do so. I also vow to take jury duty seriously if I am ever called to do it. It is our responsibility in society. My vote counts, and so does yours.

It is our civic duty to be independent thinkers and perform our own research using multiple sources. Didn't your English teacher teach you about MLA format and to cite multiple sources that only proved your point? Hello! This is another transferable skill that is quickly lost when we transition from student to society.

A factor of how our government operates typically is dependent on economics or the stock market. Different policies put in place by either party would determine the economic outcome for society. Economics as a whole is pretty straightforward. As government spending, inflation, unemployment, and consumer prices go down, consumer confidence in spending and gross domestic product (GDP) go up, and vice versa. If you're interested in economics, there are countless programs and major tracks you could pursue to specialize in it.

There are other small forms of governments within our society, which include our town or local governments. Be empowered to get involved and be the change. I know that sounds so cliché, but if anyone's going to get it done, it's us. We can prove to everyone that our generation is unstoppable, respectful, and resilient. Get involved and network within the different committees in your local town, including ones advocating for school, finance, recreation, and other critical local interests. Get involved with the particular committee that is most important to you. The tables are turning, and you are now the adults and have a civic duty to better your societies for the next generation.

Go to your school district's committee meetings and tell them what you want out of your education! Your voice matters. If you are eighteen years old and can vote for the president of the United States of America, shouldn't you have some say on your education? Ask your school committee if you can have a group of student liaisons that can discuss successful class trips, group projects, or the future of your district's education. Think about it: Most schools don't have home economics classes anymore because they actually listened to the students' feedback that it was stupid or a waste of time. The reality is that students took this class for granted. We also took the easy A for granted, too.

Now you have to read this book instead to get some feelings of the real world as you venture out into the world. Do you want a better financial understanding of what the setback is for school loans? What do you need as a down payment to buy a house? What does a budget for you look like in real life? What are the options other than going to college? Then ask for it.

It's interesting; there are obviously so many ways of handling finances, as we discussed, and there is no clear path, so maybe that's why it's not discussed in school. One model doesn't fit all people. Ask the school committee to do a student-to-society career day and have a career fair in your high school with many different options for students to be aware of. (If you do, invite me to come join!)

Take it a step further and think about how other countries operate. England has a parliament, other European countries include monarchies, and Russia has Putin! Their taxation and countries' operational structures are all different. All societies operate differently.

Taxation

Our second civic duty is understanding taxation. One way my parents taught me and my siblings about taxation at an early age came around every year at Halloween. Every Halloween, I would work really hard going door-to-door collecting candy from the neighbors. If I were operating a business, this would be income from providing a good or service. I dressed in my costume (uniform) while my parents would touch base with all the neighbors and make us say thank you. Some neighbors would give out big candy bars, and some neighbors would give out fun-sized ones. But there is typically an equal amount of work that we have to do in order to get the same results each year.

Anyways, we would come home and dump our bags of candy out on the kitchen counter. The firstborn in the family would typically categorize the candy by type, the middle child would have already started eating the candy on the way back home, and the baby in the family would probably want to rip off their costume and move onto the next activity.

I digress. We would dump the bag of candy onto the kitchen

counter, and our parents would make us pay our taxes to Uncle Sam for our earned income. Almost every year, they would teach us about taxes and take a percentage of our income that we earned that night and explain that we are citizens in a society, and we all have a duty to pay toward a collective bucket to pay for society's needs.

Everyone needs to pay taxes to make this country operate. The country needs an income. You operate as a business, your business operates as a business, and the government operates the same way. The government's income is your taxes, and its expenses are everything it takes to run the country.

My parents would explain that their income was taxed in order to support society. As citizens, federal withholdings go toward the national parks, the president's salary, the United States Armed Forces that keep us safe, and many other expenses of the government. You also pay income taxes for Medicare and Social Security.

Looking back on it, I can appreciate that they ate my candy in front of me and didn't sneak it in the middle of the night. Depending on how much candy the three of us got that night, we would each get taxed. Even if my brother walked farther than I did or scooped up extra candy from a bowl when I only took one and followed the directions left by the homeowner, my parents would tax us depending on earnings. For some reason, the Kit Kats were always taken.

That's how young I was when I learned about taxes. When did you learn about taxes? Maybe you are just starting to. Any other person with a normal childhood probably learned about taxes from their first job once they saw their first pay stub with the breakout. This is a great time to learn and to ask your parent figures about your civic duty and to research what withholdings pay for.

Then you think about taxes more. You realize there is tax on things you buy; there is tax on the money you earn; there is tax on the property you own; there is tax on the investments you have; and there are taxes on your business, and so on.

Small business owners or side-hustle entrepreneurs, who are considered the backbone of America, dreamed of having their own business someday because it is "cheaper" to have things taxed through their business rather than at the individual level, where the tax brackets are much higher. Other books will explain how business expenses are deducted before taxes, making them more beneficial than using after-tax dollars from a W-2 job. Please reference Appendix II: Book Recommendations on page 145. I would also recommend having a sophisticated accountant help you with your taxes instead of trying to do them yourself.

As you sit and read this book, I bet you're thinking, *Wow, this information is actually very informative and helpful. I will start to learn all of this once I get into the office and start a job.* That statement couldn't be more false. It is so easy to think about the first twenty years of your life. You may be thinking, *I am not really learning anything; my real learning starts once I am actually learning on the job.* That is sort of true. You will learn a bunch of stuff that you didn't learn in school on the job. There is quite a lot of information that you didn't learn in school; hence the reason for writing this book—it highlights street smarts that are equally important when you enter the workforce. That is why it is so important to take your education beyond school and take charge of it yourself with the help of this book and ones like it.

But, in defense of the treachery, you did learn a lot. You can't just start learning about taxes out of the womb. Your job for the first twenty years was to just learn and acclimate to society in some sort of school setting and develop your own skills. The real-world education you're seeking starts with a commitment to being a lifelong learner. Keep reading, watching, and exploring—your growth begins with you.

These stories are your reminder and hopefully empower you to reprogram everything and question everything for whatever your next new beginning is.

KEY TAKEAWAYS:

- **Politics Is Personal—and Powerful.** Your vote is more than a ballot—it's a voice. Understanding who and what you're voting for is part of your civic duty. Research candidates, policies, and local issues. And while it's important to stay informed, it's also wise to steer clear of political debates in professional or personal settings where mutual respect might be at risk.
- **Taxes Keep the Wheels Turning.** Whether you love them or not, taxes are a fundamental part of living in a functioning society. They fund public services, infrastructure, and safety nets. Learning how taxation works empowers you to better manage your own finances and helps you appreciate your role in the larger economic system.
- **Get Involved—Locally and Meaningfully.** Democracy doesn't end at the voting booth. Joining local boards, school committees, or community groups allows you to shape the policies and decisions that directly impact your neighborhood. Active involvement is one of the most effective ways to make your values matter—right where you live.

CHAPTER 10

NOW WHAT? THE FINAL REVIEW

The final review. It's like a final exam at the end of a semester. You were taught everything throughout the semester and were tested on what you retained or memorized. You have reviewed the key takeaways at the end of each chapter. You learned the importance of reminding clients of your added value and reviewing all that you instilled in them in order to prove your worth or bill them. Thanks for purchasing this book.

The advice now is simple: Keep tuning in to the positive voices, and keep taking in the good guidance. This is your time to put yourself first—focus on where you want to live, what you want to do, and what truly brings you joy.

All of this starts at home. It starts with showing gratitude to your family, your friends, and your partner. It starts with realizing society has slowly introduced you to different bubbles as you've gotten older and older. Yes, you are getting old. Welcome.

Then you moved to where you are right now. You are a student in a school system that is lucky to have you, and you are lucky to have them. Show gratitude for your teachers. Believe it or not, teachers' passion in life is to help teach students different topics before they make the huge transition from student to society. Beyond your family (who are biased), your teachers are the ones who have pure intentions and passion for your growth and society.

Society owes them A LOT for taking on this noble career. They also chose this career to have three summer months off during the year to have a great quality of life, but the rest of the year they love their passion for education. If you are not taking advantage of these adults who are educating you to be better people in society, you are missing the whole point. Make sure you start forming those relationships with those teachers.

After all, those teachers are the ones who you are going to need to get a recommendation letter from for whatever your future holds. Make it easy on the teacher and have an incredible impact in your community in the classroom. I'm not saying be the teacher's pet, BUT the best business that is handled in society is based on relationships. So start forming relationships and nourishing those relationships for years to come. Don't just run out of the classroom once the bell rings.

At the end of the year, write them a nice thank-you letter, especially if you are graduating soon. When you leave a job or have an interview or accept a position in the real world, you will write thank-you letters to different colleagues who you worked with because you have class. It wouldn't kill you.

Throughout your life, continue to help people. Continue to volunteer. Volunteering can sometimes feel like a punishment—like a disciplinary action—because in the real world, people are often required to do community service when they've broken the law. But volunteering shouldn't carry that kind of association.

Believe it or not, you will do a lot of volunteering in your future; you just don't know it yet. You will likely return to your high school or advanced education to donate your time to teach the next generation, give money to charities, give a discounted fee for your services to someone who just needs your help, and so on. Volunteering and doing good in the world is just good karma.

You just learned to drive, right? When you are driving in a really bad rainstorm, everyone is going the speed they are comfortable with. Everyone is staying in their own lane (hopefully). Everyone is going in different directions. The same goes for after high school. Everyone moves at their own pace and on their own timeline. While most people will eventually learn the same key life lessons, they'll do so in different ways, at different times, and through different experiences. And that's perfectly okay.

Think about your timeline after graduation and discuss it with people whose opinions you value and respect. In theory, the majority of those reading can stay on their parent figures' health insurance until they are twenty-six years old, after which they have to provide it for themselves, most likely through their full-time job! This is a really important timeline to keep in mind.

It's easy when you graduate to think, *Wow, those last four years were the best years, and they are behind me, and now I need to flip a switch and have a career right out of the gates.*

Hopefully, after reading this, you are motivated to just stay busy and connected with society and keep stacking those building blocks for your future. Frankie the Freeloader, who got the benefit of being on their parent figures' health insurance the first quarter of their life, should be grateful for that but also be mindful that one of the ticking clocks in society is when you have to cover your own health insurance, and that is one of the main reasons why everybody has a job or is married to someone who has a job because of the good health insurance benefits.

Remember to keep everything stupidly simple—in life you need shelter, water, a community, and health insurance. If you're graduating high school or college, take the opportunity to do something fun for a job that may lead to a career, especially if you can stay on your parent figures' health insurance. Do one of those jobs that you see on TikTok or Instagram where they are selling ice cream sandwiches at farmers markets on the weekends because ice cream makes people smile.

You don't necessarily have to jump into the office lifestyle to be an "adult," and who knows, maybe your makeshift summer job turns into a career where you start doing catering services at weddings and corporate events. Maybe considering yourself an adult is just when you enter society and are contributing to society in a meaningful way?

Remember, society is jealous because of your age and because of the grace society gives you because you are a child compared to them, so stay inspired and free. Eventually, you'll need to figure out the health insurance piece—but ideally, by then, your business has grown enough to absorb the cost through your earnings, or your career is stable enough.

TikTok University is raw and real. We deem anything we learn on the app practical compared to whatever we're learning in the classroom. Why are we so obsessed with seeing people on a screen be their true, raw, and authentic selves and putting it out into the world like that? When in actuality, every single one of us can do that, but we don't have to do it on a screen. We can just do it to all of the people who we come in contact with in our community, family, friends, etc. We can all be ourselves and share that with others, which will inspire them to be true and authentic to themselves.

Hopefully this book gives you more context on the rawness of this transition from student to society. Proving it doesn't happen overnight. You are the ONLY person who can say no to something. You are the only person who can say that something is not right for you or that you can't do something. You are the only limit. If you have an idea to do something, and you voice your idea to someone else, and they say, "Eh, you should stick to your day job; that's a dumb idea," don't listen. All big dreams seem dumb at first until you have figured them out. You are the only person who can say no. You won't know when to say no to something until you have tried it.

Yes, society has big expectations of the next generation, but that's only because we keep learning from the past generations' mistakes sooner, which only propels us further in society as a whole. Remember: I rise. You rise. We all rise. That said, rising together also means preparing ourselves with the tools we'll actually need. If you're wondering what kinds of real-world knowledge or life skills can help you navigate this next chapter, the following list of options is a great place to start. Consider this your starter guide—learn what you can, ask for help when you need it, and keep building as you go.

Adulting Skills

1. How to use a grill.
2. How to change a tire OR just make sure you buy a AAA membership every year for towing in case your tire pops randomly.
3. How to unclog a toilet.
4. How to sincerely apologize.

5. How to follow a recipe.
6. How to clean up after yourself.
7. How to safely use power tools.
8. How to become your own nutritionist.
9. How to meal prep or make your own lunch or family dinner.
10. How to operate a stove/oven.
11. How to do laundry.
12. How to keep track of your personal documents.
13. How to compare prices and shop smart.
14. How to take care of your skin.
15. How to declutter.
16. How to practice self-defense.
17. How to practice hand hygiene.
18. How to mow your lawn.
19. How to plan a well-rounded, educational vacation.
20. How to preserve food and know when it is going bad.
21. How to perform basic first aid and CPR.
22. How to call 911.
23. How to sew a button on.
24. How to properly make your bed.
25. How to play poker.
26. How to jump-start a car.
27. How to build a reading habit.
28. How to eat slowly.
29. How to write a check.
30. How to build a fitness routine.
31. How to have etiquette.
32. How to cope with life changes healthily.
33. How to share.

34. How to be a good friend.
35. How to put clothes away.
36. How to be adventurous.
37. How to order at a restaurant.
38. How to take the trash out.
39. How to manage social media.
40. How to protect finances.
41. How to handle documentation for a car accident.

Professional Skills

1. How to file tax returns . . . on time.
2. How to ask the right questions.
3. How to develop your soft skills.
4. How to become a financial planner.
5. How to speak to a public audience.
6. How to write a thank-you note.
7. How to write and follow up on professional emails.
8. How to accept and respond to criticism.
9. How to advocate for yourself in your job/life.
10. How to type efficiently.
11. How to decide if a topic needs an email, meeting, or phone call to get addressed properly.
12. How to master time management.
13. How to be organized.
14. How to hold eye contact when you're speaking with someone.
15. How to not be a jerk or a you-know-what.
16. How to introduce yourself in different settings.

17. How to negotiate.
18. How to order and eat at a professional meal.
19. How to master decision-making.
20. How to practice professionalism.
21. How to develop and practice problem-solving skills.
22. How to network.
23. How and when to speak up in a meeting.
24. How to communicate deliverables or tasks.
25. How to double-check your work.
26. How to be polite.
27. How to assess appropriate times to share thoughts and opinions.
28. How to deliver bad news.
29. How to have a polished conversation.
30. How to work well with others.
31. How to repeat and clarify provided directions to confirm you understood someone correctly.
32. How to both write and request a recommendation letter.
33. How to deliver an elevator pitch.

You need to realize that you are going to have a ton of transitions in your life, and this is one of them. At the time, it feels as though you have to make decisions that will last a lifetime, and they simply won't. You are growing and learning, and most of us "adults" know what it's like to be in your shoes because we have been there. All "we" want to see is some sort of effort—ask good questions and maintain a good attitude. You aren't supposed to know everything when you graduate. No one is expecting that.

Regardless of your education level, you should know life skills and how to be a good person. This is crucial for entering society. One of the most valuable yearly check-ins you can do with yourself is asking, *Am I happy enough? Am I genuinely satisfied with what I'm working on and the direction I'm heading?* That honest reflection can tell you more than any performance review ever will.

Life is supposed to be fun and full of emotion, but the greatest one that should be felt daily is happiness.

It's important to recognize which actions genuinely bring you joy—and it is just as important to notice how being around the right people can elevate that happiness even more. Even if you don't have a specific goal yet, you're still moving forward in life—and one powerful question to ask yourself along the way is, *Does this make me healthier, wealthier, or happier?* If the answer is yes to at least one, you're likely headed in the right direction.

You are still putting yourself out there every single day, and sometimes that's enough. You need to realize that and not put too much pressure on yourself. There will come a moment when you realize that you have to create the future for yourself and that the only person that is going to do it for you is you. That means you are going to have to take every necessary step toward what brings you joy in order to create wealth for yourself and a sustainable lifestyle.

When you first start thinking about your career or building your own business, you will think of the different steps that will need to take place in order to start it or grow it. Once you write all of these ideas down, no one is working for you. Your parent figures can't do it for you, and you sort of just look at the list and realize, *Wow, if I want to make this happen, if I see these things on my vision board, and I want that house and car and financial freedom, then that means I'm going to have to get my hands dirty and start doing things.* It seems so elementary. **But the difference between actually doing the work and thinking about doing the work is the difference between entrepreneurs who are making it happen and others who don't live out their dreams.**

There will not be that money tree in the backyard anymore. There will not be that trampoline that will be forgiving and bounce you back to standing when you fall. You have to create your own trampoline, your own security for yourself and for your future family. You will have the same stresses of maintaining the family as your parent figures did.

Another valuable yearly check-in? Read at least one career development book on your own time. As students, books can carry a bad connotation—assigned reading, expensive rentals, rushed chapters, quizzes, and English class nightmares. You may have even mastered the art of skimming just enough to survive being cold-called in class (bless you if you were). But here's the thing: Self-education doesn't stop after school. In the real world, you'll still need to think on your feet and "fake it 'til you make it." Pleasing your boss isn't all that different from pleasing a teacher—and let's be honest, you've been preparing for that your whole academic life.

When you're older, teaching yourself is more enjoyable. Trust me. You're learning about topics that you are interested in that are for your personal growth. Take this book for what it is. It's hopefully the first book that you will read for, DARE I SAY, pleasure, and it will inspire you to read other personal growth books that make you think as an individual. WILD. Have this book start a different relationship with books for you in the future. Have this start the reprogramming. It is a blessing to be able to give yourself access to books and learn.

Be flexible. You will not retire from your first job. You just won't.

You will have transferable skills for the next step or job in your life. You will keep expanding your network with the different industries or companies you work at. We were all secretly jealous of the new kid in high school who went to two schools and knew more people. So be that new kid and keep expanding your network. We all want to meet you and can't wait to see what you have to bring into society.

So . . . get on your way!

APPENDIX I

WORKSHEETS & EXERCISES

Personal Balance Sheets

Start today. Start on a napkin. What does your personal balance sheet look like? Think about the decisions that you'll make for your future and how they will impact your personal balance sheet positively and negatively. Mindfully, do this once a year and keep them in a book. See how things change FOR THE BETTER every year. Keep it simple. Then mock one up to focus your decisions that will get you to your goals. Keep working toward financial freedom so you can do whatever you want.

Assets
Liabilities

What Are You Good At? What Are You Not Good At?

I know what you are thinking; this chart is not busywork, though. Take a minute to write down what you are good and bad at professionally and adulting-wise. Someone will be filling this out for you in your annual review at work in the future anyway, so you might as well not feel surprised and get ahead by doing it now. Then think about what you are bad at and what you could work on, and start doing that in everyday situations, not just in class.

Good At...	Not So Good At...

Personal Wants vs. Needs

Knowing the difference between a want and a need is important. I need water, eggs, and bread. I want a Corvette and a trampoline. My mom wants me to have four children. I want one child. Drown out the noise and think about what you want and need and what others want *for* you. Knowing the difference is important as you start your life as an adult. It's your life, and you are in control of your wants and needs.

What you want in life...	What you don't want in life...	What other people want for your life...

Career Research Chart

Take time to consider your career options and how they'll impact your ideal lifestyle. Ask your network to help you understand different careers in society. The way to build wealth is finding what you love to do first; you can add a column for the salary you would range from in order to understand what it would take for planned budgeting and covering your cost of living.

Career/Job	Hours	Commute Time	Lifestyle	Certification/ Education Require-ments

Circles of Society

An illustration of the circles of society. Take a moment to fill out the names of people within each bubble who are in your society. You may even have circles within a circle to designate different groups of friends, for example.

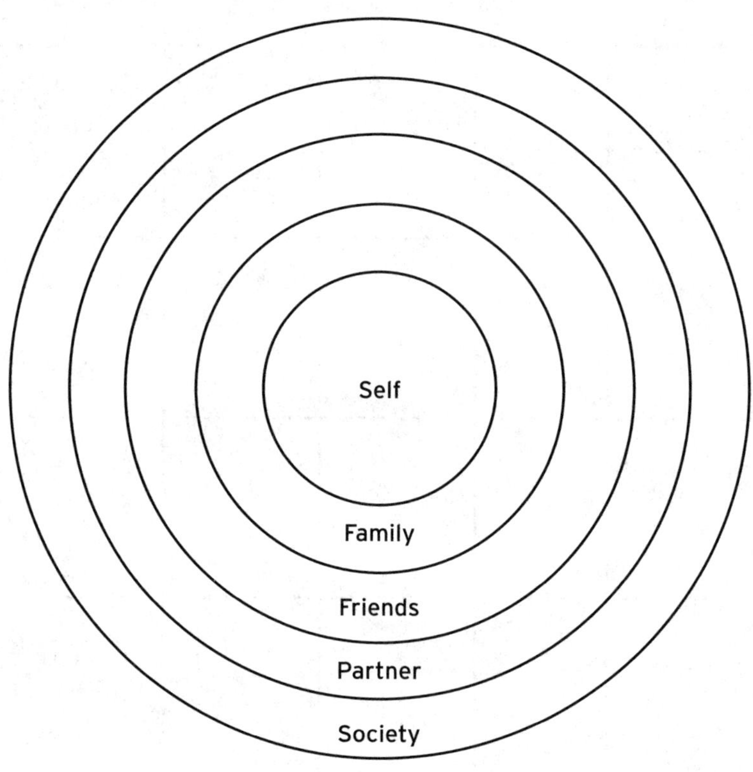

APPENDIX II

BOOK RECOMMENDATIONS

Books that I have read that spark joy while considering career and life planning.

1. *Predictable Success* by Les McKeown
2. *Financial Feminist* by Tori Dunlap
3. *Adulting for Beginners* by N. M. Hill
4. *The Mountain Is You* by Brianna Wiest
5. *The Psychology of Money* by Morgan Housel
6. *Profit First* by Mike Michalowicz
7. *How to Do the Work* by Dr. Nicole LePera
8. *Sell It Like Serhant* by Ryan Serhant
9. *The 5AM Club* by Robin Sharma
10. *The Universe Has Your Back* by Gabrielle Bernstein
11. *Working Together* by Aaron R. Cohen and Michael Eisner
12. *Freakonomics* by Stephen J. Dubner and Steven Levitt
13. *The New Gold Standard* by Joseph A. Michelli
14. *Daring Greatly* by Brené Brown
15. *Surrounded by Idiots* by Thomas Erikson
16. *Atomic Habits* by James Clear

AUTHOR'S NOTE

Many people asked me what inspired me to write this book. Honestly? I was just tired of working with people who didn't seem to have basic life or professional skills. I realized the gap wasn't always intelligence—it was often a lack of real-world guidance. So, I decided to write the kind of book I wish more people had read.

Listen, writing the book didn't stop me from dealing with stupid people, but it was a nice creative outlet for me away from my high-stress job. I wanted my future children, and frankly every child, to know I found my way through this transition, and so can they. They can find their way through society. I followed this burning passion to write this book. I would wake up in the middle of the night and think of something to write, text it to myself, and then in the morning get some sort of draft down in a Google Doc.

I think I came to the thought that everyone goes through this in life, but when does it really start? Then I reflected on my own transitions in life and came to the conclusion that the transition from student to society was the most amazing, daunting, and pivotal time in everyone's lives. I wanted students to know that there is a place for them in society. Just like me, my clients have come to the realization.

At the kitchen table with my mom, we talked about how all of these successful clients were using a lot of what they learned outside of the classroom while also pulling from things they found transferable in the classroom. We talked about how people make the world go round and how life skills or street smarts were the basis for this. We talked about how there isn't one go-to resource that lays out a wide range of jobs in one place—something a student could simply run their finger over and explore options from. It's interesting because there are so many offshoots within a career. There are so many niches. There is no way that all of these careers can be illustrated in a classroom. A career is so broad when it is described at a younger age.

I truly feel like this book is the next Dr. Seuss book, sort of like *Oh, the Places You'll Go!* It is a children's book that talks about how there are positive and negative things that happen in life, but you will still keep moving forward as long as you believe in yourself.

Sometimes the hardest part is just believing in yourself and realizing you are the only person who holds the power to tell yourself no.

To me, this book is just the beginning. I imagine taking it on tour—visiting high schools, colleges, even news stations to spread the message. I picture pep rally–style events to celebrate graduating seniors, seeing it land on summer reading lists, or even being used to kick off the school year with energy and purpose. I imagine making some sort of career encyclopedia for students to get ideas on different career options. This isn't just a book—it's a movement to prepare the next generation for real life.

In high school, we all read the same summer book, so everyone—from students to principals to lunch staff—had a shared conversation starter. I picture this book being that one day, and maybe even taking it further with summer camps and job fairs that help raise capable, confident citizens ready for what comes next.

I think about how I could be the next Guy Fieri or Mike Rowe from *Dirty Jobs* and have my own TV show while traveling the country, showcasing different students and how they run their small businesses and highlighting the emotion and drive that they have for their passion in life, while I will also show how they make their money. (If you work on a television production team, reach out to me. Let's do this. I want to monopolize like Judge Judy. What a rockstar she is!) I want to discuss how they're able to sustain their lifestyle with what they love to do and their purpose in life and then showcase how students can be inspired by them to do something similar but in their own way. It's the responsibility of the adults reading this book to help pull students into society while the students themselves are pushing forward.

The fact that my mom and I sat at the kitchen table and sketched out the table of contents for this book—simply because we saw so many people struggling with the basics after school—makes me incredibly grateful that I had the courage to just start. I didn't know exactly where it would lead, but I knew it mattered. My mom always said she wanted to write a book about life skills, so I guess I am able to do that for her with my own spin.

There is almost some false hope given to students. Here, take out some debt and take the next four years to figure it out while continuing to just be a student in the classroom. Students are missing on-the-job learning to connect their life as it is now to what they want it to be in the future. At least, that's what I feel a little robbed of. That's why internships are so important. On-the-job learning opportunities are key.

To note, I am obviously grateful for my advanced education because I have the career I have now because of it. On-the-job learning is just so crucial, and knowing the transferable skills that you learned in the classroom and applying them to the workforce is tricky to do for the first time. College is a utopia that almost sets a student back from entering society in a gradual fashion. Remember back to the beginning of the book where we talked about a school building and your employment and how they are awfully similar? College is thrown in the middle and messes with students and their transition in a way; *it's not real life*. It is just a place to gain skills to get a job.

I think about how I can help people that are just in my community and then just in my town, and then I think about all the other towns in all of the other states. Then I think about all of the other countries that have the same towns with the same small businesses with the same kids who are transitioning from student to society.

I think about the universal love and growth and evolution that we all have; I think about the universal desire to fit in and to be at home and to be happy. Personal growth is a real thing, and we are all entitled to it. Our past does not define who we can be today or tomorrow.

The biggest reason for this book is because I couldn't stop thinking about the good that this book is starting to bring. I couldn't stop thinking about the snowball effect and all it could accomplish. I hope you find something that you can't stop thinking about, too.

That's when you know you've found your place in society.

I hope this book gives you clarity. My hope is that this book has allowed you to reflect on the past and forge a path forward to success. Whatever that looks like for you. There are so many amazing things and amazing people that you haven't even met yet. There is so much good you can do in the world and in your community. You just need to go through the mud a little. I am here to tell you that's normal and okay. It will make you brave and strong. It will make you understand yourself and your place in society.

Remember, you are destined for greatness.

ABOUT THE AUTHOR

Carly MacDonald lives in a small, quiet town in New Hampshire with her husband and son. Carly specializes in preparing tax returns for small businesses and individuals and estate and trust planning. Her added value helps ensure that the money earned in the business is preserved for generations through various asset vehicles, such as trusts. This is Carly's debut book, which she wrote outside of tax season. Carly was inspired to write this book while teaching tax courses at a local college and engaging with students about their true passions and navigating how to get there. She enjoys watching TV, taking long walks, and going for rides on her quad and side-by-side in Vermont.

Where it all began: This is the outline my mom and I came up with at the kitchen counter.

Chapters

merch
daily seminars
med key chain
podcast - diff jobs

Destined for greatness

Money Management

everything your parents have taught you told by someone else

Family

Right Partner

transferable skills to real world

Fit In / Prod Citizen

Cover C of Living fin freedom

ROTH
401K

budget
careful spend for
→ can buy it but dont have to

Voting

Time Mgmt structure/routine

Personal Care & Hygiene ← portion sizes, calm yourself down, meditation

Passion / Job

Mentor

How to say no - do it make me healthy, wealthy or wiser

How to be a good friend ← secret, loyal, wake, marriage, show up for them, diff types of ppl out there - can never have too many friends

last chapter → Yearly Check In

home ec - buy new sneakers in sept
- sew
- cook
- grocery shop

ACKNOWLEDGMENTS

Thank you to the team at Amplify Publishing Group for helping me accomplish a dream that I never knew I had of writing and publishing a book. Thank you to my editor, Rebecca, for all of your hard work. You are so amazing at what you do. You have totally found your place in society. I appreciate you helping me with this dream while you are living out your own dream. Another special thank you to the graphic designer, Shannon; you knew the vision I was going for with the cover before I knew what I really wanted.